Global Investment Performance Standards (GIPS®) for Firms

Explanation of the Provisions in Section 2

February 2020

CFA Institute®
Global Investment Performance Standards

ISBN 978-1-942713-85-2

INTRODUCTION

The Explanation of the Provisions in Section 2 provides interpretation of each provision contained in Section 2: Input Data and Calculation Methodology. Firms that choose to comply with the Global Investment Performance Standards (GIPS®) must comply with all applicable requirements of the GIPS standards, including any Guidance Statements, interpretations, and Questions and Answers (Q&As) published by CFA Institute and the GIPS standards governing bodies.

Consistency of input data used to calculate performance is critical to effective compliance with the GIPS standards and establishes the foundation for full, fair, and comparable investment performance presentations. Achieving comparability among investment management firms' performance presentations requires uniformity in methods used to calculate returns. The GIPS standards mandate the use of certain calculation methodologies to facilitate comparability. The Input Data and Calculation Methodology section addresses these topics.

Each provision is included in a grey text box. Within the provisions are words appearing in small capital letters. This indicates defined terms that can be found in the GIPS Standards Glossary. Below each provision is a discussion that provides interpretive guidance to help readers understand the provision.

2. INPUT DATA AND CALCULATION METHODOLOGY

2.A. Input Data and Calculation Methodology—Requirements

Firm Assets, Composite Assets, and Pooled Fund Assets

Provision 2.A.1

TOTAL FIRM ASSETS:

a. MUST be the aggregate FAIR VALUE of all discretionary and non-discretionary assets managed by the FIRM. This includes both fee-paying and non-fee-paying PORTFOLIOS.[1]

b. MUST include assets assigned to a SUB-ADVISOR provided the FIRM has discretion over the selection of the SUB-ADVISOR.

c. MUST NOT include ADVISORY-ONLY ASSETS.

d. MUST NOT include uncalled COMMITTED CAPITAL.[2]

Discussion

Total firm assets include all discretionary and non-discretionary assets for which a firm has investment management responsibility. Total firm assets include assets assigned to a sub-advisor provided the firm has discretion over the selection of the sub-advisor. All portfolios included in total firm assets must be considered for inclusion in composites.

For periods beginning on or after 1 January 2011, firms must value all discretionary and non-discretionary assets in accordance with the definition of fair value. Fair value is defined in the GIPS standards as the amount at which an investment could be sold in an arm's-length transaction between willing parties in an orderly transaction. The valuation must be determined using the objective, observable, unadjusted quoted market price for an identical investment in an active market on the measurement date, if available. In the absence of an objective, observable, unadjusted quoted market price for an identical investment in an active market on the measurement date, the valuation must represent the firm's best estimate of the fair value. Fair value must include any accrued income.

---

[1] REQUIRED for periods beginning on or after 1 January 2011. For periods prior to 1 January 2011, TOTAL FIRM ASSETS MUST be the aggregate of either the FAIR VALUE or the MARKET VALUE of all discretionary and non-discretionary assets under management within the defined FIRM.

[2] REQUIRED for periods beginning on or after 1 January 2020.

The requirement to value all assets at fair value applies to assets in both fee-paying and non-fee-paying portfolios. Total firm assets must reflect the fair value of all discretionary and non-discretionary assets within the firm definition. For periods prior to 1 January 2011, total firm assets must be the aggregate of the fair value or market value of all discretionary and non-discretionary assets under management within the defined firm.

Some firms use a sub-advisor to manage part or all of a particular strategy. For example, if a firm specializes in managing equities, it might hire a sub-advisor to manage its fixed-income assets. If a firm has discretion over selecting (i.e., can hire and/or fire) the sub-advisor, the firm must include the assets managed by the sub-advisor in total firm assets. If the firm does not have discretion over sub-advisor selection, it must not include the sub-advised assets in total firm assets, composite assets, or pooled fund assets.

A firm retains the responsibility for its claim of compliance for all its assets, including its discretionary sub-advised assets and their reported performance. Therefore, all discretionary sub-advised assets must be treated by the firm in the same manner as assets managed internally and must be subject to the same policies and procedures as internally managed assets. If the firm intends to place reliance on information from sub-advisors, it must ensure that the records and information provided by the sub-advisor meet the requirements of the GIPS standards. For reliance on third-party records and information, please refer to Provision 1.A.26.

Total firm assets must include:

- assets for which the firm has either conditional or unconditional authority to make investment decisions,
- fee-paying assets (wherein a fee is payable to the firm for the ongoing management of a portfolio's assets) and non-fee-paying assets (wherein no fee is payable to the firm for the ongoing management of a portfolio's assets),
- assets managed outside the firm (e.g., by sub-advisors) for which the firm has asset allocation (assignment) authority (i.e., the firm has discretion over the selection of the sub-advisor), and
- cash and cash equivalents (substitutes).

Note that although non-fee-paying assets may be excluded from composites, they must be included in total firm assets.

Total firm assets must exclude:

- advisory-only assets,
- uncalled committed capital, and
- overlay exposure.

Advisory-Only Assets

Advisory-only assets are assets for which the firm provides investment recommendations and for which two conditions are met. The firm:

- has no control over implementation of investment decisions, and
- does not have trading authority over the assets.

There is an important distinction between advisory-only assets, which are excluded from total firm assets, and non-discretionary portfolios that are included in total firm assets. In the case of a non-discretionary segregated account that is included in total firm assets, the account has documented client-imposed restrictions that significantly hinder a firm from fully implementing its intended strategy. Although the account is considered non-discretionary because the intended strategy cannot be fully implemented, the firm is responsible for managing the account, including the trading of its assets. In the case of an advisory-only account, the firm does not manage the account and has no trading authority for the account. The firm offers investment advice only. Unlike non-discretionary accounts, an advisory-only account does not simply have restrictions that might prevent an intended strategy from being implemented. The firm has no direct authority to manage or trade the account. For this reason, the account must not be included in any composite and must not be included in total firm assets.

Although advisory-only assets may not be included in total firm assets, a firm may wish to report firm-wide advisory-only assets. If a firm chooses to present information on its advisory-only assets, it may present advisory-only assets as either:

- a separate value, or
- the combination of total firm assets and firm-wide advisory-only assets.

If the firm wishes to present a combination of total firm assets and firm-wide advisory-only assets, it must also present firm-wide advisory-only assets for the same periods for which the combination of total firm assets and firm-wide advisory-only assets is presented.

Uncalled Committed Capital

Committed capital is defined as pledges of capital to an investment vehicle by investors (limited partners and the general partner) or the firm and is typically drawn down over a period of time. Uncalled committed capital is the amount of capital that has not yet been drawn. For periods beginning on or after 1 January 2020, uncalled committed capital must not be included in total firm assets. Uncalled committed capital is excluded from total firm assets because it is not actively under management by the firm and there may be cases in which the committed capital is never called and will never be actively managed.

Although uncalled committed capital may not be included in total firm assets, a firm may wish to report firm-wide uncalled committed capital. If a firm wishes to present information about its uncalled committed capital, it may present uncalled committed capital as:

- a separate value, or
- the combination of total firm assets and firm-wide uncalled committed capital.

If the firm presents a combination of total firm assets and firm-wide uncalled committed capital, it must also present firm-wide uncalled committed capital for the same periods for which the combination of total firm assets and firm-wide uncalled committed capital is presented.

In certain regulatory filings, uncalled capital must be included in assets under management. Therefore, assets reported for regulatory purposes may differ from total firm assets.

For periods ending prior to 1 January 2020, firms may have included uncalled committed capital in total firm assets. If this is the case, firms are not required to restate total firm assets for periods ended prior to 1 January 2020, to remove uncalled committed capital from total firm assets.

Overlay

An overlay strategy is defined as a strategy in which the management of a certain aspect of an investment strategy is carried out separately from the underlying portfolio. Overlay strategies are typically designed either to limit or maintain a specified risk exposure that is present in the underlying portfolio or to profit from a tactical view on the market by changing a portfolio's specified risk exposure. For overlay strategies, overlay exposure is defined as the economic value for which a firm has investment management responsibility. Overlay exposure is the notional value of the overlay strategy being managed, the value of the underlying portfolios being overlaid, or a specified target exposure.

Firms must not include overlay exposure in total firm assets. However, firms may wish to present information about firm-wide overlay exposure. For overlay strategy composites, the firm is not required to present total firm assets and may instead choose to present total firm overlay exposure as of each annual period end. See Provision 4.A.15.

The following table provides examples of the type of assets that must be included in or excluded from total firm assets.

Type of Asset	Included in Total Firm Assets?	Reason
Discretionary assets for which the firm has unconditional authority to implement its strategy	Yes	Firm controls investment decisions.
Non-discretionary assets for which the firm has conditional authority to implement the strategy	Yes	Firm has limited control of investment decisions.
Non-fee-paying assets for which the firm has conditional or unconditional authority to implement the strategy	Yes	Firm has all or limited control of investment decisions.
Assets directed to a sub-advisor by the firm	Yes	Firm retains discretion over sub-advisor selection and has investment management responsibility.
Assets directed to a sub-advisor by the client	No	Firm does not retain discretion over sub-advisor selection and does not have investment management responsibility.
Assets within advisory-only client relationships	No	Firm has no control over implementation of investment decisions and no trading authority for the assets.
Uncalled committed capital	No	Firm is not actively managing uncalled committed capital and may never call the capital.
Overlay exposure	No	Firm is not managing the underlying assets.

The next table provides guidance on how to distinguish among discretionary, non-discretionary, and advisory-only assets.

Scenarios Regarding Investment Management and Trading Authority

Firm's Investment Management and Trading Authority	Type of Portfolio	Assets Included in or Excluded from Total Firm Assets
• Has authority to manage the portfolio according to a specific investment mandate • Has full trading authority for the portfolio	Discretionary	Included
• Has authority to manage the portfolio • Follows client-imposed restrictions on the management of the portfolio that prevents the portfolio from being representative of a specific investment mandate • Has full trading authority for the portfolio	Non-discretionary	Included
• Provides investment recommendations that must be approved by the client; the client may or may not accept the recommendations • Has full authority to trade the portfolio if the client approves the recommendations	Non-discretionary	Included
• Provides investment recommendations that must be approved by the client • Has no authority to trade the portfolio	Advisory-only	Excluded
• Delivers a model portfolio • Has no authority to trade the portfolio	Advisory-only	Excluded

Hedge fund structure

It is common for hedge funds to use a master-feeder structure, in which offshore and on-shore feeder funds invest in a centralized master fund. All portfolio investment activity occurs at the master fund level. Feeder funds own shares of the master fund. In a master-feeder structure, a firm may include in total firm assets either the master fund assets or the sum of the feeder fund assets.

For hedge funds registered offshore, the investment management function may be formally assigned to a third-party entity that is not actually performing the portfolio management function, and the firm may be named as having an advisory-only role. If the firm is actually performing the investment management function, however, these assets must be included in total firm assets.

Determining Discretion for Wrap Fee Portfolios, including Unified Managed Accounts (UMAs)

Wrap fee programs are offered by brokerage firms (often referred to as wrap fee sponsors). These programs give investors access to numerous investment managers through one platform. Wrap fee sponsors charge a single "wrap" or "bundled" fee for several combined services (e.g., investment management, trading, custodial, and other administrative services). An investor selects the investment manager (i.e., the firm) whose strategy appears to best suit his or her needs, and the firm assumes responsibility for managing the investor's wrap fee portfolio. The firm typically has full discretion to manage the wrap fee portfolio, and the wrap fee sponsor handles trade execution, custodial, and administrative services. For this type of wrap fee portfolio, wrap fee assets are discretionary and would be included in the firm's total firm assets.

Model delivery programs are a type of wrap fee program in which the firm does not direct trades and provides only a model portfolio to the wrap fee sponsor. From the firm's perspective, the service provided is characterized as investment advice because the firm has no control over whether the trades are executed as intended. Wrap fee assets included in model delivery programs would be considered advisory-only assets, because the firm is offering advice only and is not managing the account or directing trades. These assets would, therefore, not be included in total firm assets.

There is a type of wrap fee account called a Unified Managed Account (UMA) for which the determination of discretion, and whether or not the wrap fee portfolio should be included in total firm assets, are particularly challenging. A UMA program is similar to standard wrap fee programs in many ways. Investors have access to multiple managers through a single platform, and a single bundled fee is charged for a combination of services. The distinguishing feature of a UMA portfolio is the ability to combine multiple investment strategies into a single portfolio. A UMA portfolio may hold securities associated with multiple investment strategies and firms in one custodial or brokerage account.

Although firms generally dictate the investment strategy to be used for their designated portion of the assets in a UMA portfolio, their trading responsibilities can range from those of a standard wrap fee relationship to those of a model delivery program and often lie somewhere in between.

In a typical UMA program, the firm provides a model portfolio to the UMA platform and leaves the responsibility for executing trades to the wrap fee sponsor. In some UMA programs, the firm has discretionary authority to enter trades directly on the wrap fee sponsor's platform, although such an arrangement is not typical. It should also be noted that most UMA programs include an overlay component, whereby another firm (often the wrap fee sponsor) oversees the overall composition of, and coordinates all activity in, the wrap fee portfolio. This arrangement includes cash management (how cash will be distributed among the various firms) and asset allocation decisions (rebalancing or changing the asset allocation to each firm).

The discretion that a firm has regarding a UMA portfolio depends on the characteristics of the particular UMA program. Some UMA programs may be fully discretionary, others may have shared discretion between the wrap fee sponsor and the firm, and some may be model delivery only. Discretion may also be influenced by the presence and responsibilities of an overlay manager who may have the authority to override the firm's trading directives. Determining the level of discretion is important because it dictates whether the firm must include the UMA program assets in total firm assets. Because of the varying characteristics of different UMA programs, firms must evaluate each UMA program individually to determine whether its assets must be included in total firm assets.

The following are some factors to consider when determining whether to include UMA portfolios in total firm assets:

- The contract between the sponsor and the firm:
    - A contract that indicates that the firm has discretionary authority may suggest that the portfolios governed by the contract should be included in total firm assets. If this is the case, the level of control the firm actually has should be assessed.
    - In the case of "dual contracts," in which the firm has contracts with both the sponsor and the client, a contract with the client that specifies that the firm has discretionary authority would support including the UMA portfolios in total firm assets.
- Trading authority:
    - The firm must have trading authority for the UMA portfolios to be included in total firm assets. Some possible scenarios include the following:
        - The firm submits trades to the wrap fee sponsor's platform, but the wrap fee sponsor has final approval before execution. The firm may determine that it retains sufficient trading discretion for the wrap fee portfolios to be included in total firm assets.
        - The firm does not execute trades but has contractual assurance that the trades submitted will be executed in a timely manner and receives confirmation of execution. A firm could determine that these UMA portfolios should be included in total firm assets.
        - The wrap fee sponsor is responsible for all trading and can freely decide to deviate from the firm's trading instructions. This is an advisory-only relationship, and the UMA assets must not be included in total firm assets.

- Authority at the portfolio level:
  - If the firm is making trading decisions on a portfolio-specific basis, this scenario indicates the firm has discretion. Inclusion of UMA assets in total firm assets is likely permitted.
  - If the firm does not have access to the data necessary to make decisions at the portfolio-specific level, the firm is likely to have limited authority over the portfolio and assets would not likely qualify for inclusion in total firm assets.

Because of the complexities that often exist in determining the level of discretion for a firm's UMA assets, it is common for firms to exclude UMA assets from total firm assets and treat these assets as advisory-only assets. Firms must review all UMA programs to determine if the assets should be included in total firm assets and, if included, whether the portfolios should be included in a composite.

As described, firms have many decisions to make when establishing procedures for calculating total firm assets. Total firm assets reported for any given time period must be the same in all of the firm's GIPS Reports.

Provision 2.A.2

TOTAL FIRM ASSETS, COMPOSITE assets, and POOLED FUND assets MUST:

a. Include only actual assets managed by the FIRM.

b. Be calculated net of discretionary leverage and not grossed up as if the leverage did not exist.

Discussion

Total firm assets, composite assets, and pooled fund assets must include only actual assets managed by the firm. Assets represented by simulated, backtested, or model performance must not be included in total firm assets, composite assets, or pooled fund assets because such assets do not represent actual assets managed by the firm. Because uncalled committed capital is not considered to be actual assets managed by the firm, composite assets or pooled fund assets must not include uncalled committed capital for periods beginning on or after 1 January 2020. This is consistent with the requirement to not include uncalled committed capital in total firm assets for periods beginning on or after 1 January 2020. (See Provision 2.A.1.)

When a composite or pooled fund strategy employs discretionary leverage, the composite or pooled fund assets and total firm assets must be presented net of the discretionary leverage and not grossed up as if the leverage did not exist. Discretionary leverage refers to loans taken at the investment manager's discretion. For example, if the firm is managing a fund that has $200 million in assets and the firm chooses to borrow $50 million, the fund's net assets are $200 million and its gross assets are $250 million. Because the firm chose to lever the fund, the firm must use net assets of $200 million when calculating total firm assets.

In contrast, non-discretionary leverage refers to borrowings that are mandated by or undertaken by the client. Non-discretionary leverage is not deducted when calculating total firm assets, composite assets, or pooled fund assets. For example, if the client gave the firm $250 million to manage, of which the client has borrowed $50 million, the amount of assets included in total firm assets is $250 million. The fact that the client borrowed $50 million of the assets given to the firm does not influence the calculation of the firm's total firm assets.

Provision 2.A.3

The FIRM MUST NOT double count assets when calculating TOTAL FIRM ASSETS, COMPOSITE assets, or POOLED FUND assets.

Firms are prohibited from double counting assets when calculating total firm assets, composite assets, or pooled fund assets. If double counting is not eliminated, assets reported will be inflated and result in a misleading GIPS Report. For firms that include portfolios in more than one composite, create carve-outs, or manage portfolios that invest in the firm's pooled funds (e.g., portfolios that invest in the firm's short-term money market fund), care must be taken to ensure assets are not counted more than once.

As an example, suppose that Firm XYZ has one Eurozone fixed-income composite that contains the following three portfolios:

Portfolio 1: a pooled fund invested in Eurozone bonds with net assets of €20 million,

Portfolio 2: a second pooled fund invested in Eurozone bonds of several Eurozone countries with net assets of €30 million, and

Portfolio 3: a segregated account invested entirely in the two pooled funds already mentioned. Net assets of this segregated account are €10 million.

These three portfolios are the only portfolios within Firm XYZ. The firm asks the following questions:

- What is the correct number of portfolios in the Eurozone fixed-income composite?

  The Eurozone fixed-income composite would have three portfolios in the composite.

- What is the correct amount of composite assets in the Eurozone fixed-income composite?

  The Eurozone fixed-income composite would have three portfolios in the composite, with composite assets of €50 million. Presenting composite assets of €60 million—thus including €10 million from Portfolio 3, which is invested entirely in Portfolio 1 and Portfolio 2—is misleading, and those assets would be double counted.

Portfolio	Invested In	Net Assets (€ millions)	Composite Assets/ Firm Assets (€ millions)
1	Eurozone bonds	20	20
2	Eurozone bonds	30	30
3	Portfolios 1 and 2	10	
Total		60	50

- What is the correct amount of composite assets that should be included in total firm assets? Composite assets of €50 million would also be included in total firm assets. Total firm assets would also be €50 million.

Provision 2.A.4

COMPOSITE and POOLED FUND performance MUST be calculated using only actual assets managed by the FIRM.

Discussion

Composite and pooled fund performance must be calculated using only actual assets managed by the firm. This performance must include any sub-advised assets for which the manager has discretion when selecting the sub-advisor.

Simulated, backtested, or model performance must not be included in any composites or pooled funds because such performance does not represent actual assets managed by the firm. Similarly, firms must not blend the history of two existing composites or pooled funds to create simulated performance for a "hybrid" or model composite or pooled fund and present it as a GIPS-compliant track record. For example, if the performance of actual portfolios in an equity composite is combined with the performance of actual portfolios in a fixed-income composite to show what the results might have been had the equity and fixed-income portfolios been combined, the results would be considered a simulated strategy. This "hybrid" or model composite may be presented as supplemental information only if all of the component parts are presented. Even though the returns for the equity and fixed-income composites are based on actual assets managed by the firm, the arbitrary method of combining them historically is subject to manipulation and does not represent real-time, actual asset allocation decisions. The performance results of this simulated strategy would, therefore, be considered hypothetical performance. This would also be true for combinations of different pooled funds or carve-outs used to create a simulated strategy.

Firms may present theoretical performance in GIPS Reports. Theoretical performance is not derived from actual assets invested in the strategy presented, and it includes model, backtested, hypothetical, simulated, indicative, ex ante, and forward-looking performance. Theoretical performance must be clearly labeled as supplemental information. Firms must not link historical theoretical performance with actual performance. For example, assume a firm manages equity portfolios and fixed-income portfolios. The firm wishes to create a track record for a balanced strategy invested 50% in equities and 50% in fixed income, rebalanced monthly, but it does not manage any portfolios in this balanced strategy. The firm uses the equity composite and the fixed-income composite as building blocks to create a 50/50 blended balanced strategy. The performance of the balanced strategy is theoretical and may be presented as supplemental information when all of the underlying building block composites are presented—in this case, the equity and fixed-income composites. It must be clear, however, that the performance for the balanced strategy is theoretical performance, and the appropriate disclosures about theoretical performance must be included.

A ported composite or pooled fund track record (a track record from a past or acquired firm that meets the portability requirements and can be used by the new or acquiring firm) is considered to be an extension of the new or acquiring firm. The assets of the ported track record must be included in composite assets or pooled fund assets. While a ported track record is not based on actual assets that had been managed at the new or acquiring firm, it must be based on actual assets at the past or acquired firm.

Overlay Exposure

Provision 2.A.5

Total FIRM OVERLAY EXPOSURE MUST include all discretionary and non-discretionary OVERLAY STRATEGY PORTFOLIOS for which the FIRM has investment management responsibility.[3]

Discussion

For periods beginning on or after 1 January 2020, total firm overlay exposure must include all discretionary and non-discretionary overlay strategy portfolios for which the firm has investment management responsibility. When calculating total firm overlay exposure, firms must sum the overlay exposures of all overlay portfolios managed even if different allowable methods are used to calculate the portfolios' overlay exposure. To calculate overlay exposure, a firm may use the notional value of the overlay strategy portfolios, the value of the underlying portfolios being overlaid, or a specified target exposure. If overlay exposure is maintained in different currencies, the firm must convert the overlay exposure to the currency used in the GIPS Report. For purposes of calculating total firm overlay exposure, firms must not recalculate overlay exposures to a single method.

For example, assume Firm A offers two types of overlay strategies. In one strategy, called "Global Equity Beta Overlay," the composite overlay exposure of €500 million is calculated using the

[3] REQUIRED for periods beginning on or after 1 January 2020.

notional exposure of all portfolios in the composite at period end. In the second strategy, "Active Currency Overlay," the composite overlay exposure of €750 million is calculated using the value of the underlying portfolios at period end. Firm A would calculate total firm overlay exposure of €1,250 million by summing €500 million and €750 million.

Provision 2.A.6

When calculating OVERLAY EXPOSURE, the FIRM MUST:[4]

a. Use the notional exposure of the OVERLAY STRATEGY PORTFOLIOS, the value of the underlying PORTFOLIOS being overlaid, or a specified target exposure.

b. Use the same method for all PORTFOLIOS within a COMPOSITE.

Discussion

For periods beginning on or after 1 January 2020, there are three allowable methods for calculating overlay exposure. Overlay exposure must be calculated by using:

- the notional exposure of the overlay strategy portfolios being managed,
- the value of the underlying portfolios being overlaid, or
- a specified target exposure.

The same method for calculating overlay exposure must be used for all portfolios within a composite.

For periods ending prior to 1 January 2020, these same methods may be used, but firms are not required to use these methods.

Provision 2.A.7

When calculating OVERLAY STRATEGY PORTFOLIO returns, the FIRM MUST:[5]

a. Use as the denominator the notional exposure of the OVERLAY STRATEGY PORTFOLIOS, the value of the underlying PORTFOLIO being overlaid, or a specified target exposure.

b. Use the same method for all PORTFOLIOS within a COMPOSITE.

[4] REQUIRED for periods beginning on or after 1 January 2020.

[5] REQUIRED for periods beginning on or after 1 January 2020.

Discussion

When calculating returns for an overlay strategy portfolio, the denominator must be one of the following:

- the notional exposure of the overlay strategy portfolios as of the beginning of the period,
- the value of the underlying portfolio being overlaid as of the beginning of the period, or
- the specified target exposure as of the beginning of the period, which can be defined as a target exposure or determined by a formula used to calculate the target exposure for each period.

Some overlay strategies require the use of a specific denominator. For example, when an interest rate overlay is benchmarked to a set of cash flows, the notional amount of derivatives required to hedge the interest rate exposure will not equal the present value of the cash flows being hedged because the notional amount will vary depending on the instruments chosen to implement the hedge. An interest rate overlay return calculated by dividing the profit/loss earned by the portfolio during the period by the notional exposure of the instruments used would not be comparable to the change in present value of the cash flows being hedged. Therefore, the denominator for an interest rate overlay benchmarked to a set of cash flows must be the sum of the present value of the cash flows being hedged as of the beginning of the period.

The same method for calculating the denominator must be used for all portfolios within a composite when calculating overlay strategy portfolio returns. In addition, this same method must be used to calculate a composite's total overlay exposure.

General/Accounting

Provision 2.A.8

TOTAL RETURNS MUST be used.

Discussion

Total return, which is measured over a specified period, has two components: (1) the appreciation or depreciation (capital change) of the assets in the portfolio over the specified period and (2) the income earned on the assets in the portfolio over the specified period. When calculating the performance of a portfolio, firms are required to use a total return.

Provision 2.A.9

TRADE DATE ACCOUNTING MUST be used.[6]

Discussion

For periods beginning on or after 1 January 2005, trade date accounting must be used. For the purpose of complying with the GIPS standards, trade date accounting is defined as recognizing the asset or liability on the date of purchase or sale and not on the settlement date. Recognizing the asset or liability within three business days of the date the transaction is entered into (the trade date [T], T + 1, T + 2, or T + 3) satisfies the trade date accounting requirement for purposes of the GIPS standards. Settlement date accounting recognizes the asset or liability on the date when the exchange of cash and investments is completed.

For purchases, when using settlement date accounting, any movement in value between the trade date or booking date and the settlement date will not affect performance until the settlement date. For purchases, when using trade date accounting, the change in value will be reflected for each valuation between trade date and settlement date. Performance comparisons between portfolios and/or composites that use settlement date accounting and those that use trade date accounting may not be valid. The same problem occurs when comparing settlement date portfolios and composites with their benchmarks.

The principle behind requiring trade date accounting is to ensure there is not a significant lag between trade execution and reflecting the trade in the performance of a portfolio. For the purpose of compliance with the GIPS standards, portfolios are considered to satisfy the trade date accounting requirement provided that transactions are recorded and recognized consistently and within normal market practice—typically, a period between trade date and up to three business days after trade date (T + 3).

For some pooled funds, firms may need to differentiate between the date of placing a subscription/redemption order and the date of the effective asset ownership transfer. The date of the execution or transfer of ownership (in this case, when the definitive quantity and settlement price of the asset being purchased/sold is determined and becomes known) should be considered the trade date.

External cash flows are typically booked on the date when they are actually received or distributed. If a firm receives notification of incoming funds and trades on a pre-announced external cash inflow before it is received into the portfolio, the portfolio will become leveraged during the period between the trade date and the date when the external cash inflow is physically received. To "cover" this additional exposure and eliminate the leverage effect, firms may choose to apply

[6] REQUIRED for periods beginning on or after 1 January 2005.

the trade date and settlement date principles to pre-arranged external cash flows by booking the external cash flow with a trade date that reflects the date the firm may trade in advance of the external cash inflow and a settlement date that reflects the date when the cash is received. If the firm chooses to match the trade date of pre-announced external cash flows to the trade date of trades related to those external cash flows, it should establish this as its policy and treat all pre-announced external cash flows consistently.

Provision 2.A.10

ACCRUAL ACCOUNTING MUST be used for fixed-income securities and all other investments that earn interest income, except that interest income on cash and cash equivalents may be recognized on a cash basis. Any accrued income MUST be included in the beginning and ending PORTFOLIO values when performance is calculated.

Discussion

Accrual accounting allows the recording of financial transactions as they come into existence rather than when they are paid or settled. When determining the valuation for a security that pays interest income, firms must include the income that would have been received at the end of the performance period had the security actually paid interest income earned during the performance period.

Accrued interest income must be included in both the beginning and ending portfolio values when performance is calculated. Interest should be accrued for a security in the portfolio using whatever method is customary and appropriate for that security.

Some instruments already include accrued income as part of the security's market price. If income for these instruments is being accrued as part of the income recognition process, steps should be taken to ensure that the income is not double counted.

Income on cash and cash equivalents may be recognized on either an accrual or cash basis. Accrued income for cash and cash equivalents can be difficult to calculate. Unlike bonds with a known coupon rate, some short-term securities (e.g., overnight deposits) may not have a published interest rate. Firms must develop a methodology for accounting for short-term interest earnings and consistently apply the method selected. Firms could consider using the last actual known interest rate to accrue income for the most recent period. When the actual rate becomes known, an adjustment can then be made to allocate the actual income earned to the proper period. In this way, there is no systematic underestimation or overestimation of income, and income is also properly assigned to the period when earned. Cash-basis accounting (recording the income for short-term cash and cash equivalents as it is actually received) will tend to lag the suggested accrual method by recognizing income a month after it was earned. Either method is acceptable, however, and the method chosen must be used consistently.

An issue that may arise is how to calculate the performance of a bond, including the accrual of interest, when a bond goes into default. In this situation, the firm must recognize the loss when it occurred and the historical performance must not be recalculated. The accrual of interest must be included in the calculation method up until the point of the bond's default. At that point, the calculation method would reflect the loss of accrued interest by adjusting the amount of accrued interest to zero. When and if the bond comes out of default and there is a reasonable expectation that the bond will commence paying interest, including back interest, the firm must begin accruing for such interest payments. The firm must not allocate such payments over periods when they were originally due but not paid.

Provision 2.A.11

Returns from cash and cash equivalents MUST be included in all return calculations, even if the FIRM does not control the specific cash investment(s).

Discussion

Returns earned on cash and cash equivalents held in portfolios must be combined with the returns of other assets in the portfolio to calculate the portfolio's return. The firm's asset allocation decisions, including allocation to cash, are a component of investment strategy implementation and thus part of the portfolio's return.

If the firm does not control the actual investment of cash (e.g., cash is always invested in a custodial money market fund or invested separately by the client) but does control the amount of the portfolio that is allocated to cash, then the cash assets must be included in the firm's total assets and the performance of cash must be included in the portfolio performance.

This is true even if a client-selected cash vehicle "breaks" the $1.00 net asset value (NAV). A break occurs when the NAV of a money market fund falls below the $1.00 NAV. This scenario may happen when the money market fund's investment income does not cover operating expenses or investment losses. Because the firm chose to have portfolio assets "invested" in cash and cash equivalents, it is responsible for the performance of this investment and the change in NAV must be included in the total return of the portfolio. Additionally, the firm must continue to include the portfolio in the respective composite. The fact that the investment of cash is technically not under the firm's control will not generally affect the portfolio's returns as much as the allocation of assets to cash, which is under the firm's control.

Provision 2.A.12

Returns for periods of less than one year MUST NOT be annualized.

Discussion

Composite or pooled fund performance reflects only the performance of actual assets managed by the firm. When returns for periods of less than one year are annualized, the partial-year return is "extended" in order to create an annual return. The extrapolation of the partial-year return produces a simulated return and does not reflect the performance of actual assets. Therefore, performance for periods of less than one year must not be annualized.

Care must be taken when money-weighted returns (MWRs) are calculated and the composite or pooled fund has less than a year of performance. Many firms use Excel to calculate MWRs using the XIRR function. The XIRR function calculates an annualized internal rate of return (IRR) (an IRR is a method that can be used to calculate an MWR). When calculating an XIRR for a period of less than one year, the annualized return generated must be "de-annualized."

The non-annualized since inception IRR (SI-IRR) can be calculated as follows:

$$R_{SI\text{-}IRR} = \left[(1 + r_{SI\text{-}IRR})^{\frac{TD}{365}} \right] - 1,$$

where

$R_{SI\text{-}IRR}$ = non-annualized since-inception internal rate of return

$r_{SI\text{-}IRR}$ = annualized since-inception internal rate of return

TD = total number of calendar days in the measurement period (less than one year)

For example, a portfolio is funded with $1,000,000 cash on 1 September 2020. Another $75,000 is contributed on 10 September 2020. At the end of the month, 30 September 2020, the portfolio is valued at $1,100,000. Also assume that end-of-day cash flows are used. Using Excel's XIRR formula the annualized SI-IRR is 34.41%.

Dates	External Cash Flows & Ending Valuation		Explanation
1-Sep-2020	$	(1,000,000)	Contribution
10-Sep-2020	$	(75,000)	Contribution
30-Sep-2020	$	1,100,000	Portfolio value as of 30 September 2020
		34.41%	Calculated annualized return using XIRR

To calculate the non-annualized return in Excel, using the non-annualized SI-IRR formula, the calculation is as follows:

= (1 + 0.3441)^(29/365) – 1

= 2.38%

Provision 2.A.13

All returns MUST be calculated after the deduction of TRANSACTION COSTS incurred during the period. The FIRM may use estimated TRANSACTION COSTS only for those PORTFOLIOS for which actual TRANSACTION COSTS are not known.

Discussion

Transaction costs are defined as the costs of buying or selling investments. These costs typically take the form of brokerage commissions, exchange fees and/or taxes, and/or bid–offer spreads from either internal or external brokers. Custodial fees charged per transaction should be considered custody fees and not transaction costs. For real estate, private equity, and other private market investments, transaction costs include all legal, financial, advisory, and investment banking fees related to buying, selling, restructuring, and/or recapitalizing investments but do not include dead deal costs.

Both gross-of-fees returns and net-of-fees returns must reflect the deduction of transaction costs incurred in the purchase or sale of investments. Transaction costs must be deducted when calculating performance because these are costs that must be paid in order to implement the investment strategy. A firm may use estimated transaction costs only for those portfolios whose actual transaction costs are not known. It is the firm's responsibility to determine if there are any regulatory requirements that would prohibit the use of estimated transactions costs. If such regulatory requirements exist, estimated transaction costs must not be used.

When a portfolio's transaction costs are not known, a reasonable estimate of transactions costs (i.e., an estimate that the firm judges to be a fair approximation of actual transaction costs) may be used. Some approaches for determining a reasonable estimate of transactions costs include basing estimated transactions costs on:

- actual transaction costs for portfolios that the firm manages in the same or similar strategy, or
- actual transaction costs for similar securities that trade in a similar market.

The estimate of transaction costs may take the form of a percentage cost that can be applied to the portfolio return to determine the portfolio return after the deduction of those costs, or as a monetary value. If a monetary value is used, for costs that are based on the size of the transaction, the firm should scale the monetary transaction cost estimate sourced from a similarly managed portfolio to the monetary value of the portfolio.

For wrap fee portfolios, if the firm is able to obtain estimated transaction costs from wrap fee sponsors, it should use the highest estimated transaction costs. For the treatment of estimated transaction costs in bundled fee portfolios, please refer to Provision 2.A.14.

Regardless of the approach used, the firm must have documentation supporting the transaction costs on which the estimate is based.

Firms that use estimated transaction costs must document their policies and procedures for estimating transaction costs, along with the rationale for their method of estimating transaction costs, and apply the policies consistently. The methodology and assumptions used to estimate transactions costs must be periodically reviewed to ensure that the policies are still judged to result in a reasonable estimate of transaction costs.

Finally, in some markets brokers offer zero commission trades. If a portfolio is paying zero commissions, then it is appropriate to calculate portfolio gross-of-fees and net-of-fees returns that reflect zero transaction costs. However, the zero-transaction cost must not be used as a model transaction cost for other portfolios. When a composite includes portfolios that pay zero commissions, firms should disclose this fact. Not disclosing this fact could be misleading.

Provision 2.A.14

For PORTFOLIOS with BUNDLED FEES, if the FIRM cannot estimate TRANSACTION COSTS or if actual TRANSACTION COSTS cannot be segregated from a BUNDLED FEE:

a. When calculating GROSS-OF-FEES returns, returns MUST be reduced by the entire BUNDLED FEE or the portion of the BUNDLED FEE that includes the TRANSACTION COSTS.

b. When calculating NET-OF-FEES returns, returns MUST be reduced by the entire BUNDLED FEE or the portion of the BUNDLED FEE that includes the TRANSACTION COSTS and the INVESTMENT MANAGEMENT FEE.

Discussion

A bundled fee portfolio has a fee structure that combines multiple fees into one total or "bundled" fee. Bundled fees can include any combination of investment management fees, trading costs, custody fees, and/or administrative fees. Two examples of bundled fees are wrap fees and all-in fees. Calculations of gross-of-fees and net-of-fees returns for all portfolios, including bundled fee portfolios, must reflect the deduction of transaction costs incurred by the portfolio during the measurement period.

A gross-of-fees return is the return on investments reduced by any transaction costs incurred during the period. When calculating a bundled fee portfolio's gross-of-fees return, if the firm can identify the portion of the bundled fee that includes the transaction costs, that is the only portion of the bundled fee that must be reflected in the performance calculation. If the firm is unable to determine the portion of the bundled fee that includes the transaction costs and is unable to determine an appropriate estimate of transaction costs, then the entire bundled fee must be deducted when calculating the bundled fee portfolio's gross-of-fees return.

A net-of-fees return is the gross-of-fees return reduced by investment management fees, which include both performance-based fees and carried interest. A net-of-fees return must, therefore, reflect the deduction of both transaction costs and investment management fees. To meet the requirements of the GIPS standards when calculating a bundled fee portfolio's net-of-fees return, if the firm can identify the portion of the bundled fee that includes transaction costs and investment management fees, that is the only portion of the bundled fee that must be reflected in the performance calculation. If the firm is unable to identify the portion of the bundled fee that includes transaction costs and investment management fees, and it is unable to determine an appropriate estimate of transaction costs and an appropriate model investment management fee, then the entire bundled fee must be reflected (i.e., reduce performance) when calculating the bundled fee portfolio's net-of-fees return.

A pure gross-of-fees return is the return on investments that is not reduced by any transaction costs incurred during the period. When presenting returns for a composite of portfolios with bundled fees, it is permitted to show a pure gross-of-fees return as supplemental information.

Provision 2.A.15

All REQUIRED returns MUST be calculated net of discretionary leverage, unless otherwise specified.

Discussion

All required returns must be calculated net of discretionary leverage, unless otherwise specified. Discretionary leverage refers to loans taken at the firm's discretion. For example, suppose that a client gives the firm $1 million to manage. The firm then borrows another $500,000. The net of discretionary leverage amount (i.e., the assets on which performance is calculated) is $1 million, not $1.5 million, which is the gross of discretionary leverage amount.

In contrast, non-discretionary leverage refers to borrowings that are mandated by or undertaken by the client. For example, suppose that a client gives the firm $1.5 million to manage, of which the client has borrowed $500,000. In this case, the amount of assets on which performance is calculated is $1.5 million. The fact that the client borrowed $500,000 of the assets given to the firm does not influence the calculation of the firm's performance.

Firms that use subscription lines of credit and calculate and present since-inception money-weighted returns (MWRs) are required to present MWRs both with and without the subscription line of credit. Considering only the subscription line of credit, and ignoring any other leverage that may exist, the return with the subscription line of credit is considered a levered return and the return without the subscription line of credit would be considered an unlevered return. The one exception to the requirement to present MWRs both with and without the subscription line of credit is included in Provision 7.A.2. A firm is required to only present returns with the subscription line of credit, and not returns without the subscription line of credit, when it is presenting an MWR and the subscription line of credit has both of the following characteristics:

- The principal was repaid within 120 days using committed capital drawn down through a capital call;
- No principal was used to fund distributions.

Other than the exception for subscription lines of credit in Provision 7.A.2, the rationale for requiring that all returns be calculated net of discretionary leverage is that an unlevered return is hypothetical, and it is not appropriate for a firm to include such a return when calculating the performance of a portfolio or a composite. Unlevered performance that does not reflect the deduction of discretionary leverage is permitted to be presented only as supplemental information.

Provision 2.A.16

The FIRM MUST calculate performance in accordance with its COMPOSITE-specific or POOLED FUND–specific calculation policies.

Discussion

A firm must create composite-specific and/or pooled fund–specific policies for calculating the performance of its portfolios and composites. It must apply these policies consistently when calculating performance. A firm must ensure that its policies for calculating performance address not only assets managed internally but also those managed externally, or for which performance is calculated externally. A firm claiming compliance with the GIPS standards that uses external managers and service providers is responsible for having policies and procedures in place to ensure that the relevant outsourced services produce information on which the firm relies that is consistent with the requirements of the GIPS standards and that all GIPS standards requirements have been met.

Although it is not possible to list all of the items that must be included in a firm's policies and procedures for calculating the performance of its portfolios and any composites, the following are examples of some of the items that a firm must address in its policies and procedures relating to performance calculation:

- How the firm ensures that the information from third-party service providers meets the requirements of the GIPS standards and can be used, as necessary, to produce returns that comply with the GIPS standards;
- The policies for estimating transaction costs, if estimated transaction costs are used;
- The fees and expenses deducted when calculating gross-of-fees returns and net-of-fees returns;
- The methodology for calculating a time-weighted return (TWR) for portfolios and composites for which the firm presents a TWR;
- The methodology for calculating a money-weighted return (MWR) for portfolios and composites for which the firm presents an MWR;
- The calculation methodology for portfolios with external cash flows;
- The treatment of reclaimable withholding taxes when recording interest income and dividends;
- How model investment management fees are calculated, if used in calculating net-of-fees returns;
- The treatment of performance-based fee clawbacks, if any; and
- The treatment of side pockets, if any.

Although a firm must establish a composite-specific or pooled fund–specific calculation policy, that policy may differentiate calculations used for different types of portfolios in the composite. For example, suppose that a firm has a composite that includes pooled funds, which use a daily TWR calculation methodology, and segregated accounts, which use a Modified Dietz return (with revaluations for large cash flows) calculation methodology. The firm may have a different policy for the return calculation methodologies used for pooled funds versus segregated accounts that are included in the same composite. The firm must apply the composite-specific calculation policy consistently, however, based on the return calculation methodology for each type of portfolio in the composite.

It is possible that all of a firm's composites and pooled funds use the same calculation policy; however, the appropriate policy must be determined for each composite and/or pooled fund. The firm must not simply establish this policy on a firm-wide basis without considering whether the policy is appropriate for each composite or pooled fund.

A firm's policies and procedures for calculating performance must be designed to ensure that the firm adheres to all applicable laws and regulations regarding the calculation and presentation of performance. Firms must establish policies and procedures to ensure that performance and performance-related information does not include false or misleading information.

Policies and procedures should be reviewed regularly to determine if they should be changed or improved, but it is not expected that they will change frequently. A firm must not change a policy retroactively solely to increase performance or to present the firm in a better light. Retroactive changes to policies and procedures should be avoided.

The firm should also conduct periodic testing or other monitoring procedures to ensure that all outsourced policies and procedures are being applied consistently and appropriately.

Provision 2.A.17

For PORTFOLIOS invested in underlying POOLED FUNDS, all returns MUST reflect the deduction of all fees and expenses charged at the underlying POOLED FUND level, unless the FIRM controls the INVESTMENT MANAGEMENT FEES of the underlying POOLED FUNDS. When the FIRM controls the INVESTMENT MANAGEMENT FEES of the underlying POOLED FUNDS, the FIRM may calculate GROSS-OF-FEES returns that do not reflect the deduction of the underlying POOLED FUND INVESTMENT MANAGEMENT FEES.

Discussion

If presenting returns for portfolios invested in underlying pooled funds, all returns must reflect the deduction of all fees and expenses charged at the underlying pooled fund level, because investors must pay these fees. When the firm controls the investment management fees of the underlying pooled funds, however, it may calculate gross-of-fees returns that do not reflect the deduction of the underlying pooled fund investment management fees. An investment management fee includes both asset-based and performance-based fees. In such situations, the firm can present the gross-of-fees returns gross of the underlying funds' investment management fees but net of the underlying funds' transaction costs and other expenses. The following represent some situations in which this criterion is met:

- Both underlying funds and the fund-of-funds are managed by the same firm, and there is effectively a fee rebate or waiver at the fund-of-funds level for those fees charged at the underlying fund level.
- A fund-of-funds that resembles a master-feeder structure or a segregated portfolio that invests in one or multiple underlying funds managed by the same firm. Its investment management fee model is structured so that the investment management fee is either partially or fully charged at the underlying fund level.

Provision 2.A.18

When calculating ADDITIONAL RISK MEASURES:

a. The PERIODICITY of the COMPOSITE or POOLED FUND returns and the BENCHMARK returns MUST be the same.

b. The risk measure calculation methodology of the COMPOSITE or POOLED FUND and the BENCHMARK MUST be the same.

Discussion

Evaluating past performance requires an understanding of the risks taken to achieve the results. The firm may choose to present additional risk measures for a composite or pooled fund and for the benchmark that it determines are appropriate for the composite's or pooled fund's investment mandate, objective, or strategy. An additional risk measure is a risk measure included in a GIPS Report beyond those required to be presented. A firm may choose to present a proprietary measure of risk as an additional risk measure, but it must describe the proprietary measure of risk that is presented and explain why it was selected.

The periodicity of the composite or pooled fund and the benchmark must be identical when calculating additional risk measures. Periodicity refers to the length of the period over which a variable is measured (e.g., composite performance calculated monthly has monthly periodicity). As an example, if a firm is calculating an additional risk measure for a composite or pooled fund that has monthly returns and a benchmark that has quarterly returns, the firm would be required to use quarterly composite or pooled fund returns, not monthly returns, when calculating an additional risk measure. The firm must also determine that there are enough data points for the selected measure to be statistically significant so as not to be misleading.

It is also required that the risk measure calculation methodology of the composite or pooled fund and the benchmark be the same. Firms are required to select a calculation methodology on a composite-specific or pooled fund–specific basis, document the methodology in their policies and procedures, and consistently apply that methodology. Firms are required to maintain records supporting all calculations presented in GIPS Reports.

Valuation

Provision 2.A.19

PORTFOLIOS MUST be valued in accordance with the definition of FAIR VALUE.[7]

Discussion

The quality of a return depends on the quality of the valuations included in the calculation of that return. Performance reporting is of little value unless the underlying valuations are

[7] REQUIRED for periods beginning on or after 1 January 2011. For periods prior to 1 January 2011, PORTFOLIO valuations (excluding REAL ESTATE and PRIVATE EQUITY) MUST be based on FAIR VALUES or MARKET VALUES. For periods prior to 1 January 2011, REAL ESTATE investments MUST be valued at FAIR VALUE or MARKET VALUE (as previously defined for REAL ESTATE in the 2005 edition of the GIPS standards). For periods ending prior to 1 January 2011, PRIVATE EQUITY investments MUST be valued at FAIR VALUE, according to the GIPS Private Equity Valuation Principles in Appendix D of the 2005 edition of the GIPS standards, or the GIPS Valuation Principles in Chapter II of the 2010 edition of the GIPS standards.

based on sound valuation principles. Beginning 1 January 2011, portfolio valuations must be based on fair value.

Fair value is defined as the amount at which an investment could be sold in an arm's length transaction between willing parties in an orderly transaction. The valuation must be determined using the objective, observable, unadjusted quoted market price for an identical investment in an active market on the measurement date, if available. In the absence of an objective, observable, unadjusted quoted market price for an identical investment in an active market on the measurement date, the valuation must represent the firm's best estimate of the fair value. Fair value must include any accrued income.

As noted in the definition of fair value, when determining fair value, firms must use the objective, observable, unadjusted quoted market prices for identical investments in active markets on the measurement date, if available. Markets are not always liquid, however, and investment prices are not always objective and/or observable. For illiquid or hard-to-value investments, or for investments for which no observable market value or market price is available, additional steps are necessary. A firm's valuation policies and procedures must address situations in which the market prices may be available for similar but not identical investments, inputs to valuations are subjective rather than objective, and/or markets are inactive instead of active.

A very small number of circumstances exist in which cost or book value may be deemed to be fair value. Examples include stable value assets, such as guaranteed investment contracts (GICs) or real estate in the first year of the purchase of the property. In such cases, if a firm can support a determination that cost or book value and fair value are the same, it is acceptable for book value to be used when calculating asset values and returns.

It is important that a firm establish fair valuation policies that take into account the specific characteristics of asset classes or investment products. For example, to fair value an international pooled fund might require a firm to roll forward the valuation of the fund to the local market, in order to strike a Net Asset Value (NAV) based on more current prices than the local market close prices.

There is a recommended valuation hierarchy in provision 2.B.6. Firms are not required to follow the valuation hierarchy, but it is recommended that they do so.

Although a firm may use external third parties to value investments, the firm still retains responsibility for compliance with the GIPS standards, which includes the requirement to fairly value investments.

Over time, the type of valuation required and the minimum valuation frequency have changed. Prior editions of the GIPS standards included valuation guidance specific to private equity. The 2020 edition of the GIPS standards has no private equity–specific requirements. Instead, private equity is included in the broader category of private market investments. Please see the historical valuation requirements for various asset classes in the following exhibit.

Time Frame	Valuation Method	Minimum Valuation Frequency
Portfolios Except Private Market Investments		
1 Jan 2011 to Current	Fair Value	Monthly and on the date of all large cash flows
1 Jan 2010 to 31 Dec 2010	Fair Value or Market Value	Monthly and on the date of all large cash flows
1 Jan 2001 to 31 Dec 2009	Fair Value or Market Value	Monthly
Prior to 1 Jan 2001	Fair Value or Market Value	Quarterly
Private Market Investments (except real estate and private equity)		
1 Jan 2011 to Current	Fair Value	Quarterly
Prior to 1 Jan 2011	Fair Value or Market Value	Quarterly
Private Equity		
1 Jan 2011 to Current	Fair Value	Quarterly
1 Jan 2008 to 31 Dec 2010	Fair Value (According to the GIPS Private Equity Valuation Principles in Appendix D of the 2005 edition of the GIPS standards, or the GIPS Valuation Principles in Chapter II of the 2010 edition of the GIPS standards)	Quarterly
Prior to 1 Jan 2008	Fair Value (According to the GIPS Private Equity Valuation Principles in Appendix D of the 2005 edition of the GIPS standards, or the GIPS Valuation Principles in Chapter II of the 2010 edition of the GIPS standards)	Annually
Real Estate—Open-End Fund		
1 Jan 2011 to Current	Fair Value	Quarterly
1 Jan 2008 to 31 Dec 2010	Fair Value or Market Value (as previously defined for Real Estate in the 2005 edition of the GIPS standards)	Quarterly
Prior to 1 Jan 2008	Fair Value or Market Value (as previously defined for Real Estate in the 2005 edition of the GIPS standards)	Annually
1 Jan 2020 to Current	External Valuation	Every 12 months
1 Jan 2012 to 31 Dec 2019	External Valuation	Every 12 months unless client agreements stipulate otherwise, in which case investments must be externally valued every 36 months
1 Jan 06 to 31 Dec 2011	External Valuation	Every 36 months

(continued)

Time Frame	Valuation Method	Minimum Valuation Frequency
Real Estate—Not in an Open-End Fund		
1 Jan 2011 to Current	Fair Value	Quarterly
1 Jan 2008 to 31 Dec 2010	Fair Value or Market Value (as previously defined for Real Estate in the 2005 edition of the GIPS standards)	Quarterly
Prior to 1 Jan 2008	Fair Value or Market Value (as previously defined for Real Estate in the 2005 edition of the GIPS standards)	Annually
1 Jan 2012 to Current	External Valuation	1. External valuation every 12 months unless client agreements stipulate otherwise, in which case investments must be externally valued every 36 months; or 2. Annual financial statement audit
1 Jan 2006 to 31 Dec 2011	External Valuation	Every 36 months

Provision 2.A.20

The FIRM MUST value PORTFOLIOS in accordance with the COMPOSITE-specific or POOLED FUND–specific valuation policy.

Discussion

When daily calculations are not used, a firm must not value a portfolio "opportunistically" and must follow its composite-specific or pooled fund-specific valuation policies consistently. For example, assume that a firm's valuation policy is to value portfolios for large cash flows, defined in the composite-specific valuation policy as a single external cash flow equal to or greater than 5% of the portfolio's beginning-of-month value. For any single external cash flow that is less than 5% of the portfolio's beginning-of-month value, the firm must not value the portfolio. For any single external cash flow that is equal to or greater than 5% of the portfolio's beginning-of-month value, the firm must value the portfolio. The firm must apply the composite-specific or pooled fund–specific valuation policy consistently and not "cherry-pick" when to value portfolios.

Although a firm must establish a composite-specific valuation policy, that policy may differentiate valuation frequency for different types of portfolios in the composite. For example, suppose that a firm has a composite that includes pooled funds, which are valued daily, and segregated accounts, which are valued monthly and for external cash flows above 5%. The firm may have a different policy for the frequency of valuing pooled funds versus segregated accounts that are included in the same composite. The firm must apply the composite-specific valuation policy consistently, however, based on the valuation frequency for each type of portfolio in the composite.

It is possible that all of a firm's composites and pooled funds use the same valuation policy; however, the appropriate policy must be determined for each composite and/or pooled fund. The firm must not simply establish this policy on a firm-wide basis without considering whether the policy is appropriate for each composite or pooled fund.

A firm must ensure that its policies for calculating performance address not only assets managed internally but also those managed externally or for which performance is calculated externally. A firm claiming compliance with the GIPS standards that uses external managers and service providers is responsible for having policies and procedures in place to ensure that the relevant outsourced services produce information on which the firm relies that is consistent with the requirements of the GIPS standards and that all GIPS standards requirements have been met.

Policies and procedures should be reviewed regularly to determine if they should be changed or improved, but it is not expected that they will change frequently. A firm must not change a policy retroactively solely to increase performance or to present the firm in a better light. Retroactive changes to policies and procedures should be avoided.

The firm should also conduct periodic testing or other monitoring procedures to ensure that all outsourced policies and procedures are being applied consistently and appropriately.

Provision 2.A.21

If the FIRM uses the last available historical price or preliminary, estimated value as FAIR VALUE, the FIRM MUST:

a. Consider it to be the best approximation of the current FAIR VALUE.
b. Assess the difference between the approximation and final value and the effect on COMPOSITE or POOLED FUND assets, TOTAL FIRM ASSETS, and performance, and also make any adjustments when the final value is received.

Discussion

It is not uncommon for private market investments to be valued using preliminary, estimated values. If a firm uses the last available historical price or preliminary, estimated values as fair value, perhaps in order to produce a GIPS Report on a timely basis, the firm must consider the estimate of value to be the best approximation of the current fair value, and this must be defined in the firm's fair valuation policy. When using preliminary, estimated values, the firm should obtain an understanding of the process used to establish estimated values in order to determine whether reliance can be placed on the process.

Firms must define the use of the last available historical price or preliminary, estimated values, and the treatment of subsequent final values, in their composite-specific and/or pooled fund–specific fair valuation policies. The valuation policies must be followed consistently and made available upon request. If the firm uses the last available historical price or preliminary, estimated values, when final values are received the firm must assess the difference between the estimate of value and the final value, as well as the effect on composite or pooled fund assets, total firm assets, and performance. If the final values and resulting performance differ materially, firms must determine whether any adjustments to the composite or pooled fund must be made on a prospective basis or retroactively. If composite or pooled fund valuations are revised retroactively, firms must consider the requirements related to error correction and the firm's error correction policies. Differences between final and estimated values are not considered to be errors but are treated similarly.

It is important to remember the underlying principles of the GIPS standards: fair representation and full disclosure. If differences between the estimated and final values are consistently material, the firm should reassess whether it is proper to continue to use the estimates of fair value.

Provision 2.A.22

COMPOSITES and POOLED FUNDS MUST have consistent beginning and ending annual valuation dates. Unless the COMPOSITE or POOLED FUND is reported on a non-calendar fiscal year, the beginning and ending valuation dates MUST be at calendar year end or on the last business day of the year.[8]

Discussion

It is required that composites and pooled funds have consistent beginning and ending annual valuation dates. Such consistency will result in improved comparability of data. Unless the composite or pooled fund is reported on a non-calendar fiscal year, the beginning and ending valuation dates of the composite or pooled fund must be at calendar year end or on the last business day of the year. Portfolios in a composite must also have consistent beginning and ending valuation dates corresponding to the reporting period. If the composite or pooled fund beginning or ending annual valuation dates fall on a weekend or a holiday, the firm should use the valuation on the last business day of the period. If there is an available benchmark value on the same day as the ending valuation day for the composite or pooled fund, the firm should use the benchmark value from the ending valuation day for the composite or pooled fund. If the composite or pooled fund ending annual valuation date differs from that of the benchmark, this difference should be disclosed. For example, if the annual period end and the last valuation falls on 30 December because of the New Year's Eve holiday but the end of the annual period for the benchmark falls on

[8] REQUIRED for periods beginning on or after 1 January 2006.

31 December, any material difference in performance should be disclosed. The firm should use the benchmark value from 30 December if it is available.

Note that a firm's composites and/or pooled funds may have different year-end valuation dates if one or more of the firm's composites or pooled funds is reported on a non-calendar fiscal year, whereas other composites and/or pooled funds are reported as of calendar year end or on the last business day of the year. The annual valuation dates must correspond to the reporting dates for the composite or pooled fund. It is important, however, that the annual periods within a GIPS Report are consistent. For example, a GIPS Pooled Fund Report that reports a pooled fund's performance annually as of 30 June, its fiscal year end, must consistently report data for years ending 30 June for the pooled fund. The firm may decide in the future to create a GIPS Pooled Fund Report for the pooled fund based on a 31 December valuation and reporting date; however, the firm may not mix 30 June and 31 December annual reporting periods in the same GIPS Pooled Fund Report and must report all annual returns as of the calendar year end.

Portfolios—Time-Weighted Returns

Provision 2.A.23

When calculating TIME-WEIGHTED RETURNS for PORTFOLIOS that are included in COMPOSITES, all PORTFOLIOS except PRIVATE MARKET INVESTMENT PORTFOLIOS (see 2.A.40) MUST be valued:

a. At least monthly.[9]

b. As of the calendar month end or the last business day of the month.[10]

c. On the date of all LARGE CASH FLOWS. The FIRM MUST define LARGE CASH FLOW for each COMPOSITE to determine when PORTFOLIOS in that COMPOSITE MUST be valued.[11]

Discussion

The requirements contained in Provision 2.A.23 apply to a firm's portfolios that are included in composites, with the exception of private market investment portfolios. For the valuation requirements for private market investment portfolios, firms should refer to Provision 2.A.40 and related guidance.

---

[9] REQUIRED for periods beginning on or after 1 January 2001. For periods prior to 1 January 2001, PORTFOLIOS MUST be valued at least quarterly.

[10] REQUIRED for periods beginning on or after 1 January 2010.

[11] REQUIRED for periods beginning on or after 1 January 2010.

To improve the accuracy of time-weighted performance calculations, the GIPS standards have gradually increased the minimum required frequency of portfolio valuation from quarterly, to monthly, to the date of all large cash flows.

When calculating time-weighted returns for portfolios included in composites, all portfolios (with the exception of private market investment portfolios) must be valued at least monthly. Valuing portfolios included in the composite at different end dates does not allow for comparability of information. Firms must be consistent in defining the monthly valuation period to allow for comparability of data for all GIPS Composite Reports. It is also required that the calculation period must end on the same day as the reporting period. In other words, firms must value the portfolios included in a composite on the last day of the reporting period or the nearest business day. For periods beginning on or after 1 January 2010, firms must value portfolios as of the calendar month end or the last business day of the month.

In addition to the requirement for firms to value portfolios included in a composite at least monthly, firms are required to value all portfolios included in a composite on the date of all large cash flows, if the portfolios are not valued daily. A large cash flow, defined by the firm for each composite, is the level at which the firm determines that an external cash flow may distort performance if the portfolio is not valued. The firm must determine in advance (i.e., on an ex ante basis) what is considered to be a large cash flow on a composite-specific basis. Firms must define the amount in terms of the value of cash/asset flow or in terms of a percentage of the portfolio assets or the composite assets. Firms must also determine if a large cash flow is a single external cash flow or an aggregate of a number of external cash flows within a stated period. The determination of the large cash flow level may be influenced by a variety of factors, such as the strategy's nature, its historical and expected volatility, and its targeted cash level.

A firm must not establish a high large cash flow level solely for the purpose of reducing the number of instances when portfolios must be valued because of large cash flows. The firm also must not base the policy on the degree to which the large cash flow affects the return. The large cash flow level chosen by the firm on a composite-specific basis must represent the firm's estimate of the level of external cash flow that would potentially distort the accuracy of a portfolio's performance calculation if the portfolio is not valued at the time of the external cash flow.

It is possible that all of a firm's composites have the same level of large cash flows; however, the appropriate level must be determined for each composite. The firm must not simply establish this level on a firm-wide basis without considering whether the level is appropriate for each portfolio or composite.

Revaluing portfolios as of the close of the business day prior to a large external cash flow is acceptable if external cash flows are assumed to take place at the beginning of the day.

When applying these provisions, it should be remembered that private market investment portfolios have separate valuation requirements. Firms should refer to the valuation table included in Provision 2.A.19 for additional guidance on valuation requirements, including the valuation requirements for private market investments.

Provision 2.A.24

When calculating TIME-WEIGHTED RETURNS for all PORTFOLIOS except PRIVATE MARKET INVESTMENT PORTFOLIOS (see 2.A.41) included in COMPOSITES, the FIRM MUST:

a. Calculate returns at least monthly.[12]
b. Calculate monthly returns through the calendar month end or the last business day of the month.[13]
c. Calculate sub-period returns at the time of all LARGE CASH FLOWS, if daily returns are not calculated.[14]
d. For EXTERNAL CASH FLOWS that are not LARGE CASH FLOWS, calculate PORTFOLIO returns that adjust for daily-weighted EXTERNAL CASH FLOWS, if daily returns are not calculated.[15]
e. Treat EXTERNAL CASH FLOWS according to the FIRM'S COMPOSITE-specific policy.
f. Geometrically LINK periodic and sub-period returns.
g. Consistently apply the calculation methodology used for an individual PORTFOLIO.

Discussion

Provision 2.A.24 applies to all portfolios included in composites except private market investment portfolios. Please refer to Provision 2.A.41 for the requirements regarding the calculation of a time-weighted return (TWR) for private market investment portfolios included in composites.

TWRs measure the firm's performance and attempt to negate or neutralize the effect of external cash flows to or from the client. The GIPS standards do not require a specific method to be used to calculate TWRs but do require the return methodology to meet certain criteria.

Although it is required that TWRs be calculated at least monthly, many firms calculate daily returns. If daily returns are not calculated, a firm must calculate sub-period returns for portfolios at the time of all large cash flows in order to calculate a more accurate TWR. A large cash flow is the level at which the firm determines that an external cash flow may distort performance if the portfolio is not valued at the time of the external cash flow. A large cash flow is defined by the firm

[12] REQUIRED for periods beginning on or after 1 January 2001.
[13] REQUIRED for periods beginning on or after 1 January 2010.
[14] REQUIRED for periods beginning on or after 1 January 2010.
[15] REQUIRED for periods beginning on or after 1 January 2005.

for each composite to determine when the portfolios in that composite are to be valued for performance calculations. Firms must define the amount, for each composite, in terms of the value of the cash/asset flow or in terms of a percentage of the portfolio assets or the composite assets. Firms must also determine if a large cash flow is a single external cash flow or an aggregate of a number of external cash flows within a stated period of time.

For periods beginning on or after 1 January 2001, firms must calculate portfolio TWRs at least monthly. When calculating and presenting performance in a GIPS Composite Report, calculating returns for portfolios at different end dates does not allow for the comparability of information. Therefore, to facilitate comparability, for periods beginning on or after 1 January 2010, firms must calculate monthly returns as of the calendar month end or the last business day of the month.

The actual valuation of the portfolio's investments and calculation of return each time a large cash flow occurs will result in a more accurate TWR calculation than using either the Original Dietz method or the Modified Dietz method, but it is less accurate than a "true" TWR calculation methodology, which requires valuation and return calculation with every external cash flow.

The returns calculated for each sub-period are geometrically linked according to the following formula:

$$r_t^{TWR} = \left[(1+r_1)\times(1+r_2)\times\ldots\times(1+r_I)\right]-1,$$

where r_t^{TWR} is the time-weighted return for period t and period t consists of I sub-periods.

The chief advantage of valuing a portfolio at the time of large cash flows and calculating sub-period returns is that it calculates a better estimate than the midpoint or day-weighting methods. The major disadvantage is that it requires precise valuation of the portfolio each time a large cash flow occurs. In practice, this means that firms must have the ability to value portfolios on a daily basis. If all investments are not accurately priced for each sub-period valuation, errors generated in the return calculation may be greater than the errors caused by using the midpoint or day-weighting approximation methods. In such cases, it is important to be able to correct for errors, such as missed security splits, mispricings, and improperly booked transactions, because day-to-day compounding will not correct for them automatically if external cash flows occur.

As of 1 January 2005, the calculation of portfolio returns that adjust for daily-weighted external cash flows is required, if daily returns are not calculated. The denominator in the calculation of a TWR that adjusts for daily-weighted external cash flows reflects the weighting of external cash flows for the days they have been in the portfolio and available for investment during the period. A firm must create a composite-specific policy for the treatment of external cash flows and apply the policy consistently. Examples of acceptable methods for calculating returns that adjust for daily-weighted external cash flows are the Modified Dietz method and internal rate of return (IRR). These methods are estimates of TWRs.

Modified Dietz Method

The Modified Dietz method improves upon the Original Dietz method, which assumes that all external cash flows occur during the midpoint of the period. In an attempt to determine a more accurate return, the Modified Dietz method weights each external cash flow in the denominator by the amount of time it is held in the portfolio. The formula for estimating the TWR using the Modified Dietz method is

$$r_t^{MD} = \frac{V_t^E - V_t^B - \sum_{i=1}^{I} CF_{i,t}}{V_t^B + \sum_{i=1}^{I} \left(CF_{i,t} \times w_{i,t}\right)},$$

where

r_t^{MD} = the Modified Dietz return for the portfolio for period t

V_t^E = the ending value of the portfolio for period t

V_t^B = the beginning value of the portfolio for period t

i = the number of external cash flows (1, 2, 3, . . . I) in period t

$CF_{i,t}$ = the value of external cash flow i in period t

$w_{i,t}$ = the weight of external cash flow i in period t (assuming the external cash flow occurred at the end of the day), as calculated according to the following formula:

$$w_{i,t} = \frac{D_t - D_{i,t}}{D_t},$$

where

$w_{i,t}$ = the weight of external cash flow i in period t, assuming the external cash flow occurred at the end of the day

D_t = the total number of calendar days in period t

$D_{i,t}$ = the number of calendar days from the beginning of period t to external cash flow i

The numerator of $w_{i,t}$ is based on the assumption that the external cash flows occur at the end of the day. If external cash flows were assumed to occur at the beginning of the day, the numerator would be $[(D_t - D_{i,t}) + 1]$. A firm may choose to use a beginning-of-day or end-of-day external cash flow assumption or some combination of the two. The key is to establish a policy and treat external cash flows consistently.

The chief advantage of the Modified Dietz method is that it does not require portfolio valuation on the date of each external cash flow. Its chief disadvantage is that it provides a less accurate return than when the portfolio is valued at the time of each external cash flow. The estimate suffers most when a combination of the following conditions exists: (1) One or more large external cash flows occur, and (2) external cash flows occur during periods of high market volatility—that is, the portfolio's returns are significantly non-linear.

The following is an example of a return calculation using the Modified Dietz method. The example is for a portfolio with a beginning value of $100,000 on 31 May, an ending value of $135,000 on 30 June, and external cash flows of –$2,000 on 6 June and $20,000 on 11 June. Assume the external cash flows were reflected at the end of the day.

31 May	Beginning Value (BV)	$100,000
6 June	Cash Flow (CF)	-$2,000
11 June	Cash Flow (CF)	$20,000
30 June	Ending Value (EV)	$135,000

$$R_{\text{Modified Dietz}} = \frac{EV - BV - CF}{BV + (W \times CF)}$$

W is the weight of the external cash flow for the month. Because June has 30 days and the external cash flows were assumed to occur at the end of the day, the weights of the external cash flows are calculated as (30 – 6)/30 = 0.80 and (30 – 11)/30 = 0.6333, respectively.

$$R_{\text{Modified Dietz}} = \frac{135{,}000 - 100{,}000 - (-2{,}000 + 20{,}000)}{100{,}000 + (0.80 \times -2{,}000) + (0.6333 \times 20{,}000)}$$

$$R_{\text{Modified Dietz}} = \frac{17{,}000}{111{,}067} = 15.31\%$$

If the firm's policy was to treat external cash flows as occurring at the beginning of the day, the firm would have added one to the numerator in the weight calculation, and the weights to be multiplied by the external cash flows would be calculated as (30 – 6 + 1)/30 = 0.8333 and (30 – 11 + 1)/30 = 0.6667, respectively.

The following is an example of a return calculation using the Modified Dietz method and revaluing during the month for a large cash flow (assumed to be 10% in this example). To calculate performance for the month, we must calculate performance for the sub-periods before and after the large external cash flow and then geometrically link the sub-period returns. In this example, we use the same data as in the prior example but instead value the portfolio at the time of the large cash flow on 11 June.

31 May	Beginning Value (BV)	$100,000
6 June	Cash Flow (CF)	-$2,000
11 June	Cash Flow (CF)	$20,000
11 June	Ending Value (EV)	$125,000
30 June	Ending Value (EV)	$135,000

Sub-period 1 calculation, from 31 May through 11 June:

Because sub-period 1 has 11 days and the external cash flows are assumed to occur at the end of the day, the weight of the external cash flow on the sixth day is (11 – 6)/11 = 0.4545. The weight of the cash flow on the 11th would be zero because it is assumed to happen at the end of the day on 11 June, which is when the portfolio was revalued.

$$R_{\text{Modified Dietz (sub-period 1)}} = \frac{125{,}000 - 100{,}000 - (-2{,}000 + 20{,}000)}{100{,}000 + (0.4545 \times -2{,}000) + (0 \times 20{,}000)}$$

$$R_{\text{Modified Dietz (sub-period 1)}} = \frac{7{,}000}{99{,}091} = 7.06\%$$

Sub-period 2 calculation, from 11 June through 30 June:

$$R_{\text{Modified Dietz (sub-period 2)}} = \frac{135{,}000 - 125{,}000}{125{,}000}$$

$$R_{\text{Modified Dietz (sub-period 2)}} = \frac{10{,}000}{125{,}000} = 8.00\%$$

To calculate the monthly return, geometrically link sub-period returns 1 and 2: (1 + 0.0706) × (1 + 0.08) – 1 = 0.1563, or 15.63%.

Other formulas in addition to the Modified Dietz method for calculating approximate TWRs are also permitted.

Internal Rate of Return (IRR) Method

The IRR, which is a money-weighted return, is the implied discount rate or effective compounded rate of return that equates the present value of cash outflows with the present value of cash inflows. The IRR method is an acceptable method to use to calculate a TWR when no large cash flows occur during the sub-period. To create a TWR, the IRRs before and after the large cash flow are calculated and then linked together geometrically.

The IRR is the value of R that satisfies the following equation:

$$V_E = \sum_{i=0}^{n} CF_i (1+R)^{W_i},$$

where V_E and W_i are the same as for the Modified Dietz method.

The external cash flows, CF_i, are also the same as with the Modified Dietz method with one important exception: The value at the beginning of the period is also treated as an external cash flow—that is, $V_B = CF_0$.

The IRR is obtained by selecting values for R and solving the equation until the result equals V_E. For example, if three external cash flows (including the value at the beginning of the period) have occurred, the formula will have three terms:

$$V_E = CF_0(1+R)^{W_0} + CF_1(1+R)^{W_1} + CF_2(1+R)^{W_2}.$$

The first term deals with the first external cash flow, CF_0, which is the value of the portfolio at the beginning of the period; W_i is the proportion of the period when the external cash flow CF_i was held in the portfolio. Because CF_0 is in for the whole period, $W_0 = 1$. The larger the value of CF_i in the term, the more it will contribute to the total, but the smaller the exponent (i.e., the value of W_i), the less the term will contribute to the sum. The usual effect is that the first term, with a large CF_0 and W_0 equal to 1, will contribute far more than the other terms.

The advantages and disadvantages of the IRR method are the same as those of the Modified Dietz method. The IRR method has the additional disadvantage of requiring an iterative process solution. It is also possible to have multiple answers if both positive and negative external cash flows occur.

When calculating the TWR for portfolios, periodic and sub-period returns must be linked geometrically.

A firm must create a composite-specific policy for the treatment of external cash flows for each of its composites and must apply that policy consistently. For example, the same definition of a large cash flow must be used when evaluating a cash flow for all portfolios within the composite. Policies and procedures for the calculation methodology used for an individual portfolio must also be created and applied consistently.

Pooled Funds

Provision 2.A.25

When calculating TIME-WEIGHTED RETURNS for POOLED FUNDS that are not included in a COMPOSITE, POOLED FUNDS MUST be valued:

a. At least annually.

b. As of the calendar or fiscal year end.

c. Whenever there are subscriptions to or redemptions from the POOLED FUND.

d. As of the period end for any period for which performance is calculated.

Discussion

For some pooled funds, it may not be possible to strike a net asset value (NAV) or obtain valuations as frequently as is required of other types of portfolios, because of their illiquidity or because the pricing source does not provide the valuations on a monthly or more frequent basis.

If the underlying investments of a pooled fund that is not included in a composite do not lend themselves to monthly valuations and the fund itself is open to client cash flows only on a less frequent (e.g., quarterly) basis, it may be appropriate that valuations are performed on a less frequent than monthly basis. In all cases, valuations must be conducted at least on an annual basis and must take place as of the calendar or fiscal year end.

Although a pooled fund must be valued at least annually, the subscription and redemption cycle for the pooled fund would drive the choice of the periodicity for investment valuation and performance measurement. Therefore, in addition to the requirement for at least a valuation annually, the pooled fund must be valued whenever there are subscriptions to or redemptions from the pooled fund.

The pooled fund must also be valued as of the period end for any period for which performance is calculated.

There may be instances in which some investments in a pooled fund may not be valued because of a holiday. The firm's policy may be to not strike an NAV or value the pooled fund for that particular day because of the lack of valuations for all securities. For example, assume 31 December is a holiday in some markets and, as a result, 30% of the investments in the XYZ Fund are not valued. Assume the firm's policy is to not strike an NAV unless at least 75% of the assets are valued, so the last NAV struck is on 30 December. If the difference in performance is material, this fact should be disclosed. The firm should use the benchmark value from 30 December if it is available.

GIPS Reports must include information for annual periods. Many firms present annual returns on a calendar year basis as of 31 December but are not required to do so. For example, a firm may decide to present all performance on a fiscal year basis as of 30 June or some other month end. Firms may change their annual reporting period. For example, a firm may decide to change from calendar-year reporting as of 31 December to fiscal-year reporting as of 30 June. If the firm changes the annual reporting period, it must do so for all annual periods presented in the GIPS Report. The requirement to present returns for annual periods does not prevent the firm from presenting year-to-date returns.

Provision 2.A.26

When calculating TIME-WEIGHTED RETURNS for POOLED FUNDS that are not included in a COMPOSITE, the FIRM MUST:

a. Calculate returns at least annually.
b. Calculate annual returns through the calendar or fiscal year end or the last business day of the year.
c. Calculate sub-period returns at the time of all subscriptions and redemptions.
d. Geometrically LINK periodic and sub-period returns.
e. When calculating POOLED FUND NET RETURNS, calculate POOLED FUND NET RETURNS that are net of TOTAL POOLED FUND FEES.

Discussion

If the underlying investments of a pooled fund that is not included in a composite do not lend themselves to monthly valuations and the pooled fund itself is open to client cash flows only on a less frequent (e.g., quarterly) basis, it may be appropriate to calculate time-weighted returns (TWRs) on a less frequent than monthly basis. In all cases, returns must be calculated at least annually through the calendar or fiscal year end or through the last business day of the year.

In addition to the requirement that TWRs be calculated at least annually, sub-period returns must be calculated whenever there are subscriptions to or redemptions from the pooled fund. This means that pooled funds use a "true" TWR calculation methodology, which requires valuation and return calculation with every external cash flow. The periodic and sub-period returns must be geometrically linked according to the following formula:

$$r_t^{TWR} = \left[(1+r_1)\times(1+r_2)\times\ldots\times(1+r_I)\right]-1,$$

where r_t^{TWR} is the time-weighted return for period t and period t consists of I sub-periods.

It is also required that, when calculating pooled fund net returns, the pooled fund net returns are net of total pooled fund fees. Total pooled fund fees include all of the fees and expenses charged to the pooled fund, including investment management fees, administrative fees, and other expenses. Total pooled fund fees do not include sales charges and loads that are associated with buying or selling shares of a pooled fund.

Provision 2.A.27

The FIRM MUST establish a POOLED FUND INCEPTION DATE for each POOLED FUND to determine when the POOLED FUND'S track record begins.[16]

Discussion

For periods beginning on or after 1 January 2020, firms must establish a pooled fund inception date for each pooled fund to determine when the pooled fund's track record begins. The inception date for a broad distribution pooled fund is typically the date when the fund strikes the first net asset value (NAV). For a limited distribution pooled fund, the pooled fund inception date may be based on the following dates: (1) when investment management fees are first charged, (2) when the first investment-related cash flow takes place, (3) when the first capital call is made, or (4) when the first committed capital is closed and legally binding. When presenting money-weighted returns (MWRs) with and without a subscription line of credit, firms must clearly label or identify the period covered by each MWR that is presented.

For example, assume a pooled fund track record with the line of credit begins 1 July 2020 and represents the date of the first capital call. The pooled fund track record without the line of credit begins 16 May 2019 and represents the date of the first fund investment.

For a pooled fund, the performance start date of the track record could be different depending on whether the pooled fund is included in a composite. For example, assume a unitized pooled fund started on 19 July and strikes its first NAV on that day. If the firm includes the pooled fund in a composite, it will follow the composite's new portfolio inclusion criteria and the pooled fund will be included in the composite according to the firm's composite inclusion criteria (e.g., first full month under management). If the firm creates a GIPS Pooled Fund Report for the same fund, the inception date for calculating performance to include in the GIPS Pooled Fund Report will likely be the date the pooled fund strikes its first NAV (i.e., 19 July).

Money-Weighted Returns

Provision 2.A.28

When calculating MONEY-WEIGHTED RETURNS, the FIRM MUST value PORTFOLIOS at least annually and as of the period end for any period for which performance is calculated.

---

[16] REQUIRED for periods beginning on or after 1 January 2020. For periods prior to 1 January 2020, PRIVATE EQUITY PRIMARY FUNDS MUST be included in at least one COMPOSITE defined by VINTAGE YEAR and investment mandate, objective, or strategy. For periods prior to 1 January 2020, PRIVATE EQUITY POOLED FUNDS OF FUNDS MUST be included in at least one COMPOSITE defined by VINTAGE YEAR of the POOLED FUND OF FUNDS and/or investment mandate, objective, or strategy.

Discussion

When calculating a money-weighted return (MWR), a firm must value portfolios at least annually and as of the period end for any period for which performance is calculated. Valuations must be in accordance with the definition of fair value. A more frequent valuation is considered good business practice and is recommended.

When calculating time-weighted returns (TWRs), valuations at the time of large cash flows and at period end are needed because those valuations are inputs to the TWR calculation. In a true TWR calculation, sub-period returns are calculated either daily or at the time of each external cash flow and then geometrically linked together to derive a return for the period.

For MWRs, valuations are needed only at the end of the period being measured. In addition, many portfolios for which MWRs are calculated involve private market investments with valuations that are generally performed on a less frequent basis because they are illiquid securities. For these reasons, when calculating an MWR, firms must value portfolios at least annually and as of the period end for any period for which performance is calculated, rather than monthly and at the time of large cash flows.

More-frequent valuations are generally required for client reporting purposes and are considered good business practice.

Provision 2.A.29

When calculating MONEY-WEIGHTED RETURNS, the FIRM MUST:

a. Calculate annualized SINCE-INCEPTION MONEY-WEIGHTED RETURNS.

b. Calculate MONEY-WEIGHTED RETURNS using daily EXTERNAL CASH FLOWS.[17]

c. Include stock DISTRIBUTIONS as EXTERNAL CASH FLOWS and value stock DISTRIBUTIONS at the time of DISTRIBUTION.

d. When calculating POOLED FUND NET RETURNS, calculate POOLED FUND NET RETURNS that are net of TOTAL POOLED FUND FEES.

Discussion

A money-weighted return (MWR) is a return that reflects the change in value and the timing and size of external cash flows. One commonly used method for calculating an MWR is to calculate an internal rate of return (IRR). In general, the IRR is the implied discount rate or effective

[17] Daily EXTERNAL CASH FLOWS are REQUIRED beginning 1 January 2020. Prior to 1 January 2020, quarterly or more frequent EXTERNAL CASH FLOWS MUST be used.

compounded rate of return that equates the present value of cash outflows with the present value of cash inflows. The since-inception internal rate of return (SI-IRR) is a specific version of the IRR in which the measurement period of the MWR covers the entire investment period since inception.

Unlike when using IRR to calculate a time-weighted return (TWR), using IRR to calculate an MWR does not involve the calculation or linking of sub-period returns. A single IRR is calculated for the entire period.

The IRR is the return for which the net present value of a cash flow series is equated to zero and is calculated by solving for the return that satisfies the following equation:

$$0=\sum_{i=0}^{I} CF_i \left(1+r_{IRR}\right)^{-\left(\frac{t_i}{365}\right)},$$

where

CF_i = external cash flow i [negative values for inflows (paid-in capital) and positive values for outflows (distributions)]

i = number of external cash flows (1, 2, 3, …, I) during the measurement period

r_{IRR} = annualized internal rate of return

t_i = number of calendar days between the beginning of the measurement period and the date of external cash flow i

The SI-IRR is a special version of the IRR in which the period-end value of the investment is treated as a synthetic terminal cash outflow, calculated as follows:

$$0=\left[\sum_{i=0}^{I} CF_i \left(1+r_{SI\text{-}IRR}\right)^{-\left(\frac{t_i}{365}\right)}\right]+\left[V_E\left(1+r_{SI\text{-}IRR}\right)^{-\left(\frac{TD}{365}\right)}\right],$$

where

CF_i = external cash flow i [negative values for inflows (paid-in capital) and positive values for outflows (distributions)]

i = number of external cash flows (1, 2, 3, …, I) during the measurement period

$r_{SI\text{-}IRR}$ = annualized since-inception internal rate of return

t_i = number of calendar days between the beginning of the measurement period and the date of external cash flow i

TD = total number of calendar days in the measurement period

V_E = value of the investment at the end of the measurement period. In the case of closed-end funds, this is typically the net asset value at the end of the measurement period.

Note that the above annualized formula assumes a 365-day year convention and thus may have slight inaccuracies when the measurement period contains one or more leap years.

Firms must calculate and present the annualized SI-IRR. If the period is less than a full year, firms must present the non-annualized SI-IRR. The non-annualized SI-IRR is calculated as follows:

$$R_{SI\text{-}IRR} = \left[\left(1 + r_{SI\text{-}IRR}\right)^{\frac{TD}{365}} \right] - 1,$$

where

$R_{SI\text{-}IRR}$ = non-annualized since-inception internal rate of return

$r_{SI\text{-}IRR}$ = annualized since-inception internal rate of return

TD = total number of calendar days in the measurement period

As of 1 January 2020, external cash flows must be reflected on a daily basis when calculating an MWR, which results in a more accurate return. Using daily external cash flows means that the external cash flows are dated on the date the external cash flows occur—for example, the date of a capital call or the date of a distribution. For periods prior to 1 January 2020, firms must calculate an MWR by using quarterly or more frequent external cash flows. However, firms should use daily external cash flows in calculating an MWR prior to 1 January 2020 if daily external cash flows are available.

In dealing with legacy cash flow streams that might be dated monthly for periods prior to 1 January 2020, the firm should assume that all external cash flows occurred on a particular date in the month regardless of the actual date of the external cash flow. The same is true if external cash flows are reflected on a quarterly basis. The firm could assume that all external cash flows within the month happened on the last business day of the respective month.

For example, the following table shows the date the cash flow could be reflected for performance purposes if cash flows are not reflected daily.

		Quarterly Cash Flows		Monthly Cash Flows	
Date	**Cash Flow**	**Cash Flow**	**Date**	**Cash Flow**	**Date**
4 Jan 2017	100			100	31 Jan 2017
7 Feb 2017	100			100	28 Feb 2017
9 Mar 2017	100	300	31 Mar 2017	100	31 Mar 2017
18 Apr 2017	100			100	30 Apr 2017
1 May 2017	100			100	31 May 2017
2 Jun 2017	100	300	30 Jun 2017	100	30 Jun 2017
14 Jul 2017	100			100	31 Jul 2017
8 Aug 2017	100			100	31 Aug 2017
9 Sep 2017	100	300	30 Sep 2017	100	30 Sep 2017

(continued)

		Quarterly Cash Flows		Monthly Cash Flows	
Date	Cash Flow	Cash Flow	Date	Cash Flow	Date
4 Oct 2017	100			100	31 Oct 2017
8 Nov 2017	100			100	30 Nov 2017
1 Dec 2017	100	300	31 Dec 2017	100	31 Dec 2017

Stock distributions must be included as external cash flows and must be valued at the time of distribution. The cash flow is reflected on the date the fund distributes the money to the investor.

It is also required that, when calculating pooled fund net returns for inclusion in a GIPS Pooled Fund Report, the pooled fund net returns are net of total pooled fund fees. Total pooled fund fees include all fees and expenses charged to the pooled fund, including investment management fees, administrative fees, and other expenses. Total pooled fund fees do not include sales charges and loads that are associated with buying or selling shares of a pooled fund.

In addition to SI-IRR, firms may calculate an MWR using the Modified Dietz method over the entire period. Unlike when being used to calculate a TWR, using the Modified Dietz method to calculate an MWR does not involve the calculation or linking of sub-period returns. A single MWR is calculated for the entire time period presented.

An example follows.

Modified Dietz								
Dates (MM/DD/YYYY)	Terminal Value	Cash Flows (CF)	Day of CF/ Valuation	Weighted CF	Numerator	Denominator	Return	
31 Dec 2016		2,000,000	0	2,000,000				
8 Jan 2017		200,000	8	198,905				
24 Dec 2017		(50,000)	358	(37,748)				
20 Feb 2018		(200,000)	416	(143,053)				
6 Mar 2018		150,000	430	105,852				
11 Dec 2018		(20,000)	710	(10,281)				
25 Jun 2019		100,000	906	37,988				
3 Jul 2019		30,000	914	11,232				
14 Aug 2019		(50,000)	956	(17,283)				
21 Mar 2020		(200,000)	1,176	(39,014)				
4 Jun 2020		80,000	1,251	11,499				
22 Nov 2020		(50,000)	1,422	(1,335)				
3 Dec 2020		150,000	1,433	2,875				
31 Dec 2020	2,300,000		1,461		160,000	2,119,637	7.55%	Cumulative
Total		2,140,000		2,119,637			1.84%	Annualized

The numerator is the terminal value less the sum of the cash flows (2,300,000–2,140,000), or 160,000.

The denominator is the sum of the weighted cash flows (2,119,637).

The cumulative return is calculated as 160,000/2,119,637, or 7.55%.

To calculate the annualized return, the formula is (1 + r)^(1/n) – 1, where r is the cumulative return and n is the number of years. In this example, it would be:

= (1 + 0.0755)^(1/4) – 1

= 1.84%.

Net Returns

Provision 2.A.30

When calculating COMPOSITE NET-OF-FEES returns, INVESTMENT MANAGEMENT FEES used in the calculation MUST be either:

a. Actual INVESTMENT MANAGEMENT FEES incurred by each PORTFOLIO in the COMPOSITE, or

b. A model INVESTMENT MANAGEMENT FEE appropriate to PROSPECTIVE CLIENTS.

Discussion

For composites, a net-of-fees return is defined as the gross-of-fees return reduced by investment management fees. Investment management fees are the fees payable to the investment management firm for the ongoing management of a portfolio, and these fees include performance-based fees and carried interest. They are typically asset based (based on a percentage of assets), performance based (based on the performance of the portfolio on an absolute basis or relative to a benchmark), or a combination of the two, but they may take other forms as well.

When calculating net-of-fees returns for a composite, the investment management fees used in the calculation must be either the actual investment management fees incurred by each portfolio in the composite or a model investment management fee appropriate to prospective clients. Using either of these approaches provides a realistic representation of the expected effect of fees on performance and satisfies the GIPS standards fundamental principles of fair representation and full disclosure.

When initially calculating net-of-fees returns for historical periods using model fees, the firm must determine whether it is appropriate to use a model based on current investment management fees or the investment management fees that were in effect for the respective historical period.

The GIPS standards do not require a specific calculation methodology for accounting for investment management fees when calculating net-of-fees returns for either portfolios or composites. The firm must develop a calculation methodology that generates performance that is not misleading, presents performance fairly, and is applied consistently. The firm's choice regarding whether actual investment management fees or model investment management fees are used in calculating net-of-fees returns must be documented in the firm's policies and procedures on a composite-specific basis. The firm must also document whether current or historical model fees are used for historical periods when initially calculating net-of-fees returns.

Provision 2.A.31

If the FIRM uses model INVESTMENT MANAGEMENT FEES to calculate COMPOSITE NET-OF-FEES returns, the returns calculated MUST be equal to or lower than those that would have been calculated using actual INVESTMENT MANAGEMENT FEES.

Discussion

A firm may use model investment management fees to calculate composite net-of-fees returns. When calculating net-of-fees returns using model investment management fees, the model fees should reflect current fees. When initially calculating net-of-fees returns for historical periods, the firm must determine whether it is appropriate to use current fees or the fees that were in effect for the respective historical period. In all cases, net-of-fees returns calculated using model fees must result in net-of-fees returns that are equal to or lower than those that would have been calculated if actual investment management fees had been used. In other words, firms cannot enhance their net returns by switching from actual to model fees.

The model investment management fee must be appropriate to prospective clients. There are times when using the investment management fee that is appropriate to prospective clients as a model fee results in net-of-fees returns that are not equal to or lower than those that would have been calculated using actual investment management fees. If this is the case, to ensure this provision is met, the firm will need to use a model investment management fee that is higher than the current fee that is appropriate to prospective clients. When there are multiple investment management fee schedules, the appropriate model fee used to calculate composite net-of-fee returns may be the highest investment management fee that any prospective client would pay.

A firm may wish to include a second net-of-fees return in a GIPS Report that is created using a model fee specific to a prospective client. If this second net-of-fees return does not meet the requirement of being either equal to or lower than the return that would have been calculated using actual investment management fees, this second net-of-fees return must be labeled as supplemental information. In addition, there must be a disclosure explaining how the firm arrived at the return.

Provision 2.A.32

When calculating POOLED FUND NET RETURNS, TOTAL POOLED FUND FEES used in the calculation MUST be either:

a. Actual TOTAL POOLED FUND FEES, or

b. A model TOTAL POOLED FUND FEE appropriate to PROSPECTIVE INVESTORS.

Discussion

A pooled fund net return is defined as the pooled fund gross return reduced by all fees and costs, including investment management fees, administrative fees, and other costs. Pooled fund net returns do not reflect the deduction of sales charges and loads that are associated with buying or selling shares of a pooled fund.

When calculating a pooled fund net return, a firm may use either actual total pooled fund fees or a model total pooled fund fee appropriate to prospective investors. The firm may use the total expense ratio as the model total pooled fund fee, if the total expense ratio includes all fees and costs. If the total expense ratio does not include all fees and costs, such as performance-based fees, the firm must also deduct the additional fees and costs when calculating pooled fund net returns. Using either actual total pooled fund fees or a model total pooled fund fee appropriate to pooled fund prospective investors provides a realistic representation of the expected effect of fees on the pooled fund's returns and satisfies the GIPS standards fundamental principles of fair representation and full disclosure.

When initially calculating pooled fund net returns for historical periods using model fees, the firm must determine whether it is appropriate to use current total pooled fund fees or the total pooled fund fees that were in effect for the respective historical period.

The GIPS standards do not require a specific calculation methodology for accounting for total pooled fund fees when calculating net-of-fees returns for pooled funds. The firm must develop a calculation methodology that generates performance that is not misleading, presents performance fairly, and is applied consistently. The firm's choice regarding whether the actual total pooled fund fees or a model total pooled fund fee are used in calculating pooled fund net returns must be documented in the firm's policies and procedures on a pooled fund–specific basis. When using model fees, the firm must also document whether current or historical fees are used for historical periods when initially calculating pooled fund net returns.

Firms have the following options when calculating pooled fund net returns using actual fees where the pooled fund has multiple share classes:

- Deduct from the pooled fund gross return the highest total pooled fund fee of any individual share class in the fund.
- Calculate pooled fund net returns using a weighted average of actual pooled fund net returns from all share classes.

Different pooled fund share classes may be issued to differentiate among certain investor groups for tax reasons and/or to allow for different fee structures. In some situations, it may be impossible to definitively determine which total pooled fund fee is the highest among the share classes within the pooled fund, such as when each share class has a mix of fixed and performance-based investment management fees. In this instance, it is acceptable to use the model total pooled fund fee that is applicable to the specific pooled fund prospective investor, as long as doing so results in pooled fund net returns that are equal to or lower than those that would have been calculated if using actual (effectively charged) total pooled fund fees. (See Provision 2.A.33.)

The same concept applies when there are multiple series within a share class. Assuming there are multiple series within Share Class A, and the firm is presenting pooled fund net returns based on Share Class A, the firm should either present a weighted net return of all series within Share Class A or reduce the gross return by the total pooled fund fees from the oldest or initial series to reflect the performance a prospective investor would have received had the investor been invested in the pooled fund since its inception. The firm may take either approach as long as doing so results in pooled fund net returns that are equal to or lower than those that would have been calculated if using actual (effectively charged) total pooled fund fees. (See Provision 2.A.33.)

Although a firm must disclose if model or actual fees are used to calculate pooled fund net returns, when net returns are not straightforward and/or have multiple assumptions, additional disclosure about pooled fund net return calculations may be needed to ensure that the principle of full disclosure is met.

Provision 2.A.33

If the FIRM uses model TOTAL POOLED FUND FEES to calculate POOLED FUND NET RETURNS, the returns calculated MUST be equal to or lower than those that would have been calculated using actual TOTAL POOLED FUND FEES.

Discussion

A firm may use model total pooled fund fees to calculate pooled fund net returns. When calculating pooled fund net returns using model total pooled fund fees, the model fees should reflect current fees. When initially calculating pooled fund net returns for historical periods, the firm must determine whether it is appropriate to use current total pooled fund fees or the total pooled fund fees that were in effect for the respective historical period. In all cases, pooled fund net returns calculated using model total pooled fund fees must result in pooled fund net returns that are equal to or lower than those that would have been calculated if actual total pooled fund fees had been used. In other words, firms cannot enhance their net returns by switching from actual to model fees.

The model total pooled fund fee must be appropriate to prospective investors. There are times when using the total pooled fund fee that is appropriate to prospective investors as a model fee results in net returns that are not equal to or lower than those that would have been calculated using actual total pooled fund fees. If this is the case, to ensure this provision is met, the firm will need to use a model total pooled fund fee that is higher than the current fee that is appropriate to prospective investors. When there are multiple total pooled fund fee schedules, the appropriate model fee may be the highest total pooled fund fee that any prospective investor would pay.

A firm may wish to include a second net return in a GIPS Report that is created using a model fee specific to a prospective investor. If this second net return does not meet the requirement of being either equal to or lower than the return that would have been calculated using actual total pooled fund fees, the second net return must be labeled as supplemental information. In addition, there must be a disclosure explaining how the firm arrived at the return.

Provision 2.A.34

When calculating COMPOSITE NET-OF-FEES returns and POOLED FUND NET RETURNS, the FIRM MUST reflect any PERFORMANCE-BASED FEE CLAWBACK in the period in which it is repaid.[18]

Discussion

A clawback is the repayment of previously earned performance-based fees resulting from subsequent underperformance. Beginning 1 January 2020, when calculating composite net-of-fees returns or pooled fund net returns, any performance-based fee clawback must be reflected in the period in which the firm determines previously earned performance fees must be repaid. A firm

[18] REQUIRED for periods beginning on or after 1 January 2020.

must not restate returns to eliminate performance-based fees that were previously reflected in returns.

Typically, performance fees reward positive outperformance, whereas no fee is charged when negative excess returns occur. Some performance fee models specify a penalty (negative fee) that must be paid by the manager in the case of negative excess returns, or they may require clawbacks wherein the manager must pay back the performance fee received in the past in the case of underperformance.

The firm may not restate historical net-of-fees performance because of performance fee clawbacks. The clawback is not an error correction of the performance fees accrued and crystallized in the previous periods but represents an actual penalty for the investment manager for underperforming in the current period. Restating historical performance would be misleading. In addition, in the case of pooled funds the performance fee accrued in the previous periods would already have affected the past tradable net asset value (NAV) at which investors subscribed/redeemed fund units. Restating the NAV and performance of prior periods may result in legal obligations toward investors who may need to be compensated for the NAV price differences. Such compensation would be appropriate only in the case of a retrospective error correction. In such a case, the firm must comply with its error correction policies.

Composite Returns

Provision 2.A.35

COMPOSITE TIME-WEIGHTED RETURNS except PRIVATE MARKET INVESTMENT COMPOSITES (see 2.A.42) MUST be calculated at least monthly.[19]

Discussion

The more frequently composite returns are calculated, the more accurate the results will be. Quarterly composite calculations are permitted for periods prior to 1 January 2010; subsequently, composite returns must be calculated at least monthly. The portfolios included in the composite must be consistent for the entire performance measurement period (e.g., for the entire month if the composite is calculated using monthly portfolio returns).

[19] REQUIRED for periods beginning on or after 1 January 2010. For periods beginning on or after 1 January 2006 and ending prior to 1 January 2010, COMPOSITE returns MUST be calculated at least quarterly.

Private market investment composites are excluded from this provision because they are not required to be valued monthly.

Provision 2.A.36

COMPOSITE TIME-WEIGHTED RETURNS MUST be calculated by using one of the following approaches:

a. Asset-weighting the individual PORTFOLIO returns using beginning-of-period values;

b. Asset-weighting the individual PORTFOLIO returns using a method that reflects both beginning-of-period values and EXTERNAL CASH FLOWS; or

c. Using the aggregate method.

Discussion

A composite is defined as an aggregation of one or more portfolios managed according to a similar investment mandate, objective, or strategy. The objective in calculating the composite's return is to use a method that will conceptually produce the same value as if the assets of all the individual portfolios in the composite were aggregated and a return is calculated as if the composite were one portfolio.

The GIPS standards are based on the principle of asset-weighted composite returns. For example, if a composite contains two portfolios, one of which is 10 times the size of the other, the rate of return for the larger portfolio should have more of an effect on the composite return than the rate of return for the smaller portfolio. The asset-weighted return methods satisfy this principle by weighting each portfolio's contribution to the composite rate of return by its beginning value (as a percentage of the composite's beginning value) or by its beginning value plus weighted external cash flows (as a percentage of the composite's beginning value plus weighted external cash flows). The GIPS standards require asset weighting of the portfolio returns within a composite by using beginning-of-period values, by using beginning-of-period values plus weighted external cash flows, or by aggregating portfolio assets and external cash flows to calculate performance as a single master portfolio.

When calculating composite returns for a specific period, only portfolios that are included in the composite for the entire performance period are included in the calculation. For example, when calculating monthly composite returns, only those portfolios that are managed on a discretionary basis for the full month are included in the composite return calculation. Portfolios that begin during the month, close during the month, or are otherwise determined to not qualify for inclusion in the composite for the full month must not be included in the composite return calculation. If a firm wishes to include in composite returns portfolios that do not have a full month of performance, the firm must calculate composite returns more frequently than monthly (e.g., daily). Assuming a firm calculates composite returns daily, the firm would include in the daily composite return calculation only those portfolios that were managed for the full day. Firms must create and document policies and procedures for calculating composite returns and follow those policies and procedures consistently.

The following are examples of methods that a firm may use when asset-weighting individual portfolio returns when calculating composite time-weighted returns.

The *Beginning Assets Weighting* method for calculating composite returns, R_t, uses the formula

$$R_t = \frac{\sum_{k=1}^{K}\left(V_{k,t}^{B} \times r_{k,t}\right)}{\sum_{k=1}^{K} V_{k,t}^{B}},$$

where

R_t = the beginning assets weighted return for the composite for period t

k = the number of portfolios (1, 2, 3, . . . , K) in the composite at the beginning of period t

$V_{k,t}^{B}$ = the beginning value of portfolio k for period t

$r_{k,t}$ = the return of portfolio k for period t

The Beginning Assets Weighting method can also be expressed as

$$R_t = \sum_{k=1}^{K}\left(\frac{V_{k,t}^{B}}{\sum_{k=1}^{K} V_{k,t}^{B}} \times r_{k,t}\right) = \sum_{k=1}^{K} w_{k,t}^{B} r_{k,t},$$

where $w_{k,t}^{B}$ is the weight of the value of portfolio k as a fraction of total composite asset value based on beginning asset values for period t and can be calculated according to the following formula:

$$w_{k,t}^{B} = \frac{V_{k,t}^{B}}{\sum_{k=1}^{K} V_{k,t}^{B}}.$$

The *Beginning Assets Plus Weighted External Cash Flow* method represents a refinement to the Beginning Assets Weighting method. Consider the case in which one of two portfolios in a composite doubles in value as the result of a contribution on the third day of a performance period. Under the Beginning Assets Weighting method, this portfolio would be weighted in the composite based solely on its beginning value (i.e., not including the contribution). The Beginning Assets Plus Weighted External Cash Flow method resolves this problem by including the effect of external cash flows in the calculation. Assuming that external cash flows occur at the end of the day, the weighting factor for each external cash flow is calculated using the same methodology as in the Modified Dietz method as follows:

$$w_{i,k,t} = \frac{D_t - D_{i,k,t}}{D_t},$$

where

$w_{i,k,t}$ = the weight of external cash flow i in portfolio k in period t, assuming the external cash flow occurred at the end of the day

D_t = the total number of calendar days in period t

$D_{i,k,t}$ = the number of calendar days from the beginning of period t to external cash flow i in portfolio k

The numerator of $w_{i,k,t}$ is based on the assumption that the external cash flows occur at the end of the day. If external cash flows were assumed to occur at the beginning of the day, the numerator would be $[(D_t - D_{i,k,t}) + 1]$. A firm may choose to use a beginning-of-day or end-of-day external cash flow assumption or some combination of the two. The key is to establish a policy and treat external cash flows consistently.

The Beginning Assets Plus Weighted External Cash Flow composite return can be calculated as follows:

$$R_t = \frac{\sum_{k=1}^{K}\left\{\left[V_{k,t}^{B} + \sum_{i=1}^{I_k}\left(CF_{i,k,t} \times w_{i,k,t}\right)\right] \times r_{k,t}\right\}}{\sum_{k=1}^{K}\left[V_{k,t}^{B} + \sum_{i=1}^{I_k}\left(CF_{i,k,t} \times w_{i,k,t}\right)\right]},$$

where

R_t = the beginning assets plus weighted external cash flow composite return for period t

$V_{k,t}^{B}$ = the beginning value of portfolio k for period t

i_k = the number of external cash flows $(1, 2, 3, \ldots, I_k)$ in portfolio k

$CF_{i,k,t}$ = the ith external cash flow in portfolio k for period t

$w_{i,k,t}$ = the weight of external cash flow i in portfolio k for period t

$r_{k,t}$ = the return for portfolio k for period t

The Beginning Assets Plus Weighted External Cash Flow composite return method can also be expressed by the following formula:

$$R_t = \sum_{k=1}^{K} \left(\frac{V_{k,t}}{\sum_{k=1}^{K} V_{k,t}} \times r_{k,t} \right),$$

where

R_t = the beginning assets plus weighted external cash flow composite return for period t

$r_{k,t}$ = the return for portfolio k for period t

$V_{k,t}$ = the beginning value plus weighted external cash flows of portfolio k for period t, as calculated by the following formula:

$$V_{k,t} = V_{k,t}^{B} + \sum_{i=1}^{I_k} \left(CF_{i,k,t} \times w_{i,k,t} \right),$$

where

$V_{k,t}$ = the value of portfolio k's beginning assets plus weighted external cash flows for period t

$V_{k,t}^{B}$ = the beginning value of portfolio k for period t

i_k = the number of external cash flows (1, 2, 3, . . . , I_k) in portfolio k

$CF_{i,k,t}$ = the ith external cash flow in portfolio k for period t

$w_{i,k,t}$ = the weight of external cash flow i in portfolio k for period t

The *Aggregate Return* method combines all the composite assets and external cash flows before any calculations occur to calculate returns as if the composite were one portfolio. Therefore, unlike the Beginning Assets Weighting method or the Beginning Assets Plus Weighted External Cash Flow method, the Aggregate Return method does not use portfolio returns.

The following examples show how to calculate a composite return using the Beginning Assets Weighting method, the Beginning Assets Plus Weighted External Cash Flow method, and the Aggregate Return method, assuming that external cash flows occur at the end of the day.

Composite Return

Beginning Assets Weighting method:

Portfolio	BMV	Portfolio Weight	Portfolio Return	Weighted Return
A	450,000	17.08%	12.00%	2.05%
B	785,000	29.79%	14.00%	4.17%
C	1,400,000	53.13%	11.00%	5.84%
Total	2,635,000	100.00%		12.06%

$$R_{BMV} = \frac{(450{,}000 \times 0.12) + (785{,}000 \times 0.14) + (1{,}400{,}000 \times 0.11)}{(450{,}000 + 785{,}000 + 1{,}400{,}000)} = 12.06\%$$

Beginning Assets Plus Weighted External Cash Flow method:

Portfolio	BMV	Weighted Cash Flows	BMV plus Wtd CFs	BMV plus Wtd CFs	Portfolio Return	Weighted Return
A	450,000	75,000	525,000	18.95%	12%	2.27%
B	785,000	120,000	905,000	32.67%	14%	4.57%
C	1,400,000	(60,000)	1,340,000	48.38%	11%	5.32%
Total	2,635,000	135,000	2,770,000	100.00%		12.17%

$$R_{BMV+CF} = \frac{[(450{,}000 + 75{,}000) \times 0.12] + [(785{,}000 + 120{,}000) \times 0.14] + [(1{,}400{,}000 - 60{,}000) \times 0.11]}{(450{,}000 + 75{,}000 + 785{,}000 + 120{,}000 + 1{,}400{,}000 - 60{,}000)} = 12.17\%$$

Aggregate Return method (using Modified Dietz method):

(Assuming the large cash flow level is established at the composite level, and none of the cash flows qualify as a large cash flow)

Portfolio	BMV	EMV	Cash Flows	Weighted CFs	Portfolio Return
A	450,000	665,000	150,000	75,000	12%
B	785,000	1,140,000	240,000	120,000	14%
C	1,400,000	1,440,000	(120,000)	(60,000)	11%
Total	2,635,000	3,245,000	270,000	135,000	

Composite Return ($R_{Aggregate}$) = (Total EMV – Total BMV – Total CF)/(Total BMV + Total Wtd CF)

$$R_{Aggregate} = \frac{(3{,}245{,}000 - 2{,}635{,}000 - 270{,}000)}{(2{,}635{,}000 + 135{,}000)} = 12.27\%.$$

When using the aggregate method, a manager may encounter a situation in which the composite return falls outside the range of portfolio-level returns for a given period. This scenario can occur if the policies used to calculate portfolio-level returns do not flow through to the aggregate composite-level return calculation policies. "Flowing through" to the composite means that if any portfolio is valued during the month because of a large cash flow, the entire composite would also be valued and the sub-period return calculated for both the portfolio and the composite. A firm may establish large cash flow policies, however, such that only those portfolios in the composite that experience a large cash flow during the month are valued at the time of the large cash flow and any portfolios that did not experience a large cash flow are not valued during the month. In such a situation, the composite return may be outside the range of portfolio-level returns for a given period. To prevent this situation from occurring, the firm should consider establishing a policy wherein all portfolios in the composite are valued if any portfolio in the composite is valued during the month because of large cash flows. Once a firm has established large cash flow policies for a composite, the firm must apply the large cash flow policies consistently.

Provision 2.A.37

COMPOSITE GROSS-OF-FEES returns MUST reflect the deduction of TRANSACTION COSTS.

Discussion

Transaction costs are the costs of buying or selling investments. These costs typically take the form of brokerage commissions, exchange fees and/or taxes, and/or bid–offer spreads from either internal or external brokers. Custodial fees charged per transaction should be considered custody fees, not transaction costs. For real estate, private equity, and other private market investments, transaction costs include all legal, financial, advisory, and investment banking fees related to buying, selling, restructuring, and/or recapitalizing investments but do not include dead deal costs. When calculating composite gross-of-fees returns, transaction costs must be deducted from the underlying portfolio returns.

Other fees or expenses, such as custody fees, may also be deducted. If this is the case, the firm must disclose which additional fees or costs have been deducted when calculating the gross-of-fees returns.

For additional information on deduction of transaction costs, please refer to Provision 2.A.13.

Provision 2.A.38

COMPOSITE NET-OF-FEES returns MUST reflect the deduction of TRANSACTION COSTS and INVESTMENT MANAGEMENT FEES.

Discussion

Transaction costs are the costs of buying or selling investments. These costs typically take the form of brokerage commissions, exchange fees and/or taxes, and/or bid–offer spreads from either internal or external brokers. Custodial fees charged per transaction should be considered custody fees and not transaction costs. For real estate, private equity, and other private market investments, transaction costs include all legal, financial, advisory, and investment banking fees related to buying, selling, restructuring, and/or recapitalizing investments but do not include dead deal costs.

For portfolios invested in underlying pooled funds, the firm must deduct all fees and expenses charged at the underlying pooled fund level, unless the firm controls the investment management fees of the underlying pooled funds. When the firm controls the investment management fees of the underlying pooled funds, the firm may calculate gross-of-fees returns that do not reflect the deduction of the underlying investment management fees.

Investment management fees are the fees payable to the investment management firm for the ongoing management of a portfolio. They are typically asset based (based on a percentage of assets), performance based (based on the performance of the portfolio on an absolute basis or relative to a benchmark), or a combination of the two, but they may take other forms as well. Investment management fees also include carried interest. A net-of-fees return is the gross-of-fees return from which investment management fees are deducted. Therefore, composite net-of-fees returns must reflect the deduction of both transaction costs and investment management fees.

The GIPS standards do not require a specific calculation methodology for accounting for investment management fees when calculating net-of-fees returns for either portfolios or composites. The firm must develop a calculation methodology that generates performance that is not misleading, presents performance fairly, and is applied consistently.

Provision 2.A.39

When calculating COMPOSITE MONEY-WEIGHTED RETURNS, the FIRM MUST calculate COMPOSITE returns by aggregating the PORTFOLIO-level information for those PORTFOLIOS included in the COMPOSITE.

Discussion

When calculating composite money-weighted returns, a firm is required to aggregate the portfolio-level information for all portfolios included in the composite. This method combines the assets and external cash flows from all portfolios in the composite, so the return is calculated as if the composite were one portfolio. The following example shows how since-inception internal rates of return (SI-IRRs) can be calculated for a composite that includes multiple portfolios.

In 2019, the composite includes only Fund 1. The composite SI-IRR will be based solely on the cash flows and terminal value of Fund 1. In 2020, Fund 2 joins the composite, and at the end of 2020, the two-year annualized SI-IRR will be based on the combined cash flows and terminal values of Funds 1 and 2. In 2021, Fund 3 joins the composite, and at the end of 2021, the three-year annualized SI-IRR will be based on the combined cash flows and terminal values of Funds 1, 2, and 3.

	A	B	C	D	E	F	G
1							
2					Combined		Combined
3	Date	CF or TV	Fund 1	Fund 2	Fund 1 & 2	Fund 3	Fund 1, 2 & 3
4	31-Dec-2018	Cash Flow	(1,000,000)		(1,000,000)		(1,000,000)
5	15-Jan-2019	Cash Flow	(10,000)		(10,000)		(10,000)
6	31-Dec-2019	Terminal Value	1,090,000				
7	15-Feb-2020	Cash Flow		(5,000,000)	(5,000,000)		(5,000,000)
8	30-Jun-2020	Cash Flow		(1,000,000)	(1,000,000)		(1,000,000)
9	31-Dec-2020	Terminal Value	1,100,000	6,500,000	7,600,000		
10	12-Feb-2021	Cash Flow				(4,000,000)	(4,000,000)
11	15-Mar-2021	Cash Flow	500,000				500,000
12	31-Dec-2021	Terminal Value	900,000	6,700,000		4,200,000	11,800,000
13							
14							
15							
16	Year	IRR Calc	Formula				
17	2019	7.92%	=XIRR(C4:C6,A4:A6,0.1)				
18	2020	8.47%	=XIRR(E4:E9,A4:A9,0.1)				
19	2021	7.33%	=XIRR(G4:G12,A4:A12,0.1)				

Private Market Investments

Provision 2.A.40

When calculating TIME-WEIGHTED RETURNS for PRIVATE MARKET INVESTMENT PORTFOLIOS that are included in COMPOSITES, PRIVATE MARKET INVESTMENT PORTFOLIOS MUST be valued:

a. At least quarterly.[20]

b. As of each quarter end or the last business day of the quarter.[21]

[20] REQUIRED for periods beginning on or after 1 January 2008.

[21] REQUIRED for periods beginning on or after 1 January 2010.

Discussion

A portfolio is considered a private market investment portfolio when it has an investment objective to invest primarily in private market investments. Private market investments include real assets (e.g., real estate, insurance-linked securities, collectibles, and infrastructure), private equity, and similar investments that are illiquid, not publicly traded, and not traded on an exchange.

Investments that are not private market investments must be valued at least monthly and at the time of large cash flows. Because of the illiquidity of private market investments, private market investments that are included in composites must be valued at least quarterly if time-weighted returns are being calculated, and they are not required to be valued at the time of large cash flows. Firms may use the Modified Dietz method to calculate the quarterly return. Firms are not required to value private market investment portfolios at the time of large cash flows but may do so. The firm must establish a composite-specific valuation policy, but that policy may specify a different valuation frequency for different types of portfolios in the composite. There may also be cases in which a firm may establish different valuation frequency policies for the same types of portfolios within a composite. For example, the firm may have a private market investment portfolio in a composite that provides for monthly subscriptions and redemptions, and the firm's policy is to value this portfolio monthly. Another portfolio in this same composite may have the same structure but provides for quarterly subscriptions and redemptions, and so the firm values this portfolio quarterly. The firm must apply the composite-specific valuation policy consistently based on the specified valuation frequency for the portfolios in the composite, but that policy may differentiate valuation frequency for different types of portfolios in the composite. For example, segregated accounts may be valued quarterly, whereas pooled funds are valued monthly. The firm must apply the composite-specific valuation policy consistently based on the valuation frequency for the type of portfolio.

In all cases, however, each private market investment portfolio in the composite must be valued at quarter end or on the last business day of the quarter.

Quarterly valuations are important for investors to be able to compare performance with private market investment benchmarks, which are typically not updated monthly. Quarterly valuations are also needed for comparability with other asset classes and for comparability of data in GIPS Reports. This quarterly valuation requirement can be met by either internal or external valuations.

Private market investments include real estate. For periods prior to 1 January 2008, real estate investments must be valued at least once every 12 months. The annual valuation requirement for periods prior to 1 January 2008 can be met either by internal or external valuations. An internal valuation is a firm's best estimate of value based on the most current and accurate information available to the firm. Internal valuation methodologies can include applying a discounted cash flow model, using a sales comparison or replacement cost approach, or conducting a review of all significant events (both general market events and asset-specific events) that could have a material effect on the investment. External valuations for real estate are discussed in Provisions 2.A.43 and 2.A.44.

Provision 2.A.41

When calculating TIME-WEIGHTED RETURNS for PRIVATE MARKET INVESTMENT PORTFOLIOS that are included in COMPOSITES, the FIRM MUST:

a. Calculate returns at least quarterly.[22]
b. Calculate quarterly returns through the calendar quarter end or the last business day of the quarter.[23]
c. Calculate PORTFOLIO returns that adjust for daily-weighted EXTERNAL CASH FLOWS.[24]
d. Treat EXTERNAL CASH FLOWS according to the FIRM'S COMPOSITE-specific policy.
e. Geometrically LINK periodic and sub-period returns.
f. Consistently apply the calculation methodology used for an individual PORTFOLIO.

Discussion

A portfolio is considered a private market investment portfolio when it has an investment objective to invest primarily in private market investments.

Private market investments include real assets (e.g., real estate, insurance-linked securities, collectibles, and infrastructure), private equity, and similar investments that are illiquid, not publicly traded, and not traded on an exchange.

Because private market investments do not trade publicly like stocks and bonds do, the return calculation requirements differ for private market investments. The portfolio calculation frequency is aligned with the minimum valuation frequency, which is quarterly; therefore, firms must calculate portfolio returns at least quarterly.

As of 1 January 2010, firms must calculate quarterly returns through the calendar quarter end or the last business day of the quarter when calculating time-weighted returns (TWRs) for private market investment portfolios included in composites. Consistency in return calculation dates will result in improved comparability of data for all GIPS Reports.

Because most portfolios within a composite experience external cash flows, which can often be unpredictable and are usually client driven, it is important that the calculation of portfolio TWRs adjust for daily-weighted external cash flows that occur during the calculation period. This is required for periods beginning on or after 1 January 2010. When calculating TWRs that adjust for daily-weighted external cash flows, periodic and sub-period returns must be geometrically linked.

Private market investments do not trade publicly like marketable securities do, and thus they do not have valuations readily available on a monthly basis or at the time of external cash flows.

[22] REQUIRED for periods beginning on or after 1 January 2008.
[23] REQUIRED for periods beginning on or after 1 January 2010.
[24] REQUIRED for periods beginning on or after 1 January 2010.

Therefore, firms are not required to value private market investment portfolios and to calculate sub-period returns at the time of large cash flows and to geometrically link these sub-period returns to calculate monthly TWRs, as is required for portfolios that are not private market investment portfolios. Instead, firms must calculate returns for private market investment portfolios at least quarterly and may use methods that adjust for daily-weighted external cash flows, such as the Modified Dietz or the internal rate of return (IRR) methods.

As explained in the discussion for Provision 2.A.24, the Modified Dietz and IRR methods are money-weighted return methods. By means of geometric linking of the periodic Modified Dietz or IRR returns, TWRs can be approximated. Firms must create composite-specific policies with respect to the methodology used in calculating returns for private market investment portfolios and must apply these policies consistently to the individual portfolios included in the composite.

Provision 2.A.42

COMPOSITE TIME-WEIGHTED RETURNS for PRIVATE MARKET INVESTMENT COMPOSITES MUST be calculated at least quarterly.

Discussion

Composite time-weighted returns for private market investment composites must be calculated at least quarterly. Quarterly returns are important for investors to be able to compare performance with private market investment benchmarks, which are typically reported on a quarterly basis. Quarterly returns are also needed for comparability with other asset classes and for comparability of data in GIPS Reports.

Real Estate

Provision 2.A.43

REAL ESTATE investments in a REAL ESTATE OPEN-END FUND MUST have an EXTERNAL VALUATION at least once every 12 months.[25]

[25] REQUIRED for periods beginning on or after 1 January 2020. For periods beginning on or after 1 January 2012 and ending prior to 1 January 2020, REAL ESTATE investments MUST have an EXTERNAL VALUATION at least once every 12 months unless client agreements stipulate otherwise, in which case REAL ESTATE investments MUST have an EXTERNAL VALUATION at least once every 36 months or per the client agreement if the client agreement REQUIRES EXTERNAL VALUATIONS more frequently than every 36 months. For periods beginning on or after 1 January 2006 and ending prior to 1 January 2012, REAL ESTATE investments MUST have an EXTERNAL VALUATION at least once every 36 months.

Discussion

An open-end fund is a pooled fund in which the number of investors is not fixed and the fund is open for subscriptions and redemptions. An open-end fund is considered a real estate open-end fund when it has an investment objective to invest primarily in real estate. An open-end fund that invests in any real estate and uses a real estate benchmark is also considered a real estate open-end fund.

Real estate investments include wholly owned or partially owned:

- investments in land, including products grown from the land (e.g., timber, crops),
- buildings under development, completed buildings, and other structures or improvements,
- equity-oriented debt (e.g., participating mortgage loans), and
- private interest in a property for which some portion of the return to the investor at the time of investment is related to the performance of the underlying real estate.

The following investments are not considered real estate investments, and portfolios that have these investments must follow the provisions of the GIPS standards that are not related to real estate:

- publicly traded real estate securities,
- mortgage-backed securities (MBS) and commercial mortgage-backed securities (CMBS), and
- private debt investments, including commercial and residential loans for which the expected return is solely related to contractual interest rates without any participation in the economic performance of the underlying real estate.

In addition to the requirement to fair value quarterly, real estate investments in a real estate open-end fund are required to have an external valuation at least once every 12 months.

An external valuation is an assessment of value performed by an independent third party who is a professionally designated or certified commercial property valuer or appraiser. In markets where these professionals are not available, steps must be taken to ensure that only qualified independent property valuers or appraisers are used. For additional information regarding an external valuation, please refer to Provision 2.A.45.

An external valuation is not required for a property when the property is under a sales contract and the firm believes that the sale will be finalized.

Provision 2.A.44

REAL ESTATE investments that are not in a REAL ESTATE OPEN-END FUND MUST:[26]

a. Have an EXTERNAL VALUATION at least once every 12 months unless client agreements stipulate otherwise, in which case REAL ESTATE investments MUST have an EXTERNAL VALUATION at least once every 36 months or per the client agreement if the client agreement REQUIRES EXTERNAL VALUATIONS more frequently than every 36 months; or

b. Be subject to an annual financial statement audit performed by an independent public accounting firm. The REAL ESTATE investments MUST be accounted for at FAIR VALUE, and the most recent audited financial statements available MUST contain an unmodified opinion issued by an independent public accounting firm.

Discussion

This provision applies to all real estate investments that are not included in a real estate open-end fund, including real estate investments held in a multi-asset-class portfolio. This provision does not apply to real estate that may be held by pooled funds in which the firm invests.

Real estate investments include wholly owned or partially owned:

- investments in land, including products grown from the land (e.g., timber, crops),
- buildings under development, completed buildings, and other structures or improvements,
- equity-oriented debt (e.g., participating mortgage loans), and
- private interest in a property for which some portion of the return to the investor at the time of investment is related to the performance of the underlying real estate.

The following investments are not considered to be real estate investments and must follow the provisions of the GIPS standards that are not related to real estate:

- publicly traded real estate securities,
- mortgage-backed securities (MBS) and commercial mortgage-backed securities (CMBS), and
- private debt investments, including commercial and residential loans in which the expected return is solely related to contractual interest rates without any participation in the economic performance of the underlying real estate.

[26] REQUIRED for periods beginning on or after 1 January 2012. For periods beginning on or after 1 January 2006 and ending prior to 1 January 2012, REAL ESTATE investments MUST have an EXTERNAL VALUATION at least once every 36 months or be subject to annual financial statement audit performed by an independent public accounting firm.

In addition to the requirement to fair value quarterly, real estate investments that are not in a real estate open-end fund must have either:

- an external valuation: an assessment of value performed by an independent third party who is a professionally designated or certified commercial property valuer or appraiser. In markets where these professionals are not available, steps must be taken to ensure that only qualified independent property valuers or appraisers are used; or
- a financial statement audit: an audit of a segregated account's or pooled fund's financial statements that includes the real estate investments.

If a firm chooses an external valuation to satisfy this requirement, the real estate investments must have an external valuation at least every 12 months unless client agreements stipulate a different frequency for external valuations. For example, if a client agreement stipulates that external valuations will take place every 24 months, the real estate investments in the portfolio must have an external valuation completed at least once every 24 months. Regardless of the terms of the client agreement, each real estate investment must have an external valuation at least once every 36 months. Firms are encouraged to discuss the importance of external valuation with their clients, because valuation is the major element used in the return calculation and the external appraisal typically provides a point of reference for subsequent internal valuations performed by the firm. A firm may not always be successful in convincing its clients to move to more frequent external valuations because typically the client pays the cost of the appraisal. In many markets, however, the cost of obtaining external appraisals, including subsequent updates, are not significant because of technological advances as well as increased availability of market data. For additional information regarding an external valuation, please refer to Provision 2.A.45.

Firms that opt to have an external valuation are not required to obtain an external valuation for a property when the property is under a sales contract and the firm believes that the sale will be finalized.

Instead of an external valuation, a firm may choose to have a financial statement audit. The audit must be performed by an independent, qualified (i.e., professionally designated, certified, or licensed) accounting firm. The accounting firm chosen must be knowledgeable of the accounting rules and principles that apply to the firm's financial statements, including all relevant laws and regulatory requirements. The financial statement audit may be at either the property level or portfolio level.

Although the most recent financial statement audit does not need to be through the most recent period for which the firm is claiming compliance with the GIPS standards, a financial statement audit must be performed annually. The real estate investments must be accounted for at fair value, and the most recent audited financial statements available must contain an unmodified opinion issued by the independent public accounting firm.

Provision 2.A.45

EXTERNAL VALUATIONS for REAL ESTATE investments MUST be performed by an independent third party who is a professionally designated or certified commercial property valuer or appraiser. In markets where these professionals are not available, the FIRM MUST take necessary steps to ensure that only qualified independent property valuers or appraisers are used.

Discussion

An external valuation must be performed by an independent third party who is a professionally designated or certified commercial property valuer/appraiser. In Europe, Canada, and parts of Southeast Asia, the predominant professional designation is that of the Royal Institution of Chartered Surveyors (RICS). In the United States, the professional designation is Member of the Appraisal Institute (MAI). In Australia, the designation is Certified Practicising Valuer from the Australian Property Institute. In markets where these professionals are unavailable, steps must be taken to ensure that only qualified independent valuers or appraisers are used. Even if no credentialed professionals are available, it would be unusual to not find a well-qualified independent valuer or appraiser who can value a property in a particular market.

The external valuation process must adhere to practices of the relevant valuation governing and standard setting body. Although appraisal standards may allow for a range of estimated values, it is recommended that a single value (final value conclusion) be obtained from external valuers or appraisers because only one value can be used for performance reporting.

Provision 2.A.46

The FIRM MUST NOT use EXTERNAL VALUATIONS for REAL ESTATE investments when the valuer's or appraiser's fee is contingent upon the investment's appraised value.

Discussion

The firm must not use external valuations when the valuer's or appraiser's fee is contingent upon the investment's appraised value. To do so could damage the objectivity of the valuer or appraiser and lead to a higher valuation than would otherwise be the case. The linking of a valuer's or appraiser's fee to the investment's appraised value will also lead to the perception that the investment's appraised value may have an upward bias, reducing the confidence of those evaluating the investment and the resulting valuation.

Carve-Outs

Provision 2.A.47

When calculating NET-OF-FEES returns of COMPOSITES containing CARVE-OUTS, the INVESTMENT MANAGEMENT FEES for the CARVE-OUTS MUST be representative of the INVESTMENT MANAGEMENT FEES charged or that would be charged to the PROSPECTIVE CLIENT:

a. When presenting performance to a PROSPECTIVE CLIENT for a standalone PORTFOLIO, the INVESTMENT MANAGEMENT FEE MUST be representative of the INVESTMENT MANAGEMENT FEES for a standalone PORTFOLIO managed according to that strategy.

b. When presenting performance to a PROSPECTIVE CLIENT for a multi-asset strategy PORTFOLIO, the INVESTMENT MANAGEMENT FEE MUST be representative of the INVESTMENT MANAGEMENT FEES for a multi-asset strategy PORTFOLIO managed according to that strategy.

Discussion

A carve-out is a portion of a portfolio that is by itself representative of a distinct investment strategy. It is used to create a track record for a narrow mandate from a multi-strategy portfolio managed to a broader mandate. For example, an equity composite may include the equity portions of balanced accounts wherein these equity portions are managed according to the same investment strategy as standalone portfolios.

For a composite that includes carve-outs, the presentation of performance to a prospective client must adhere to the fundamental GIPS standards principle of fair representation. The net-of-fees performance for a composite that includes carve-outs that is presented to a prospective client for a standalone portfolio must be calculated using an investment management fee that is representative of the investment management fees for a standalone portfolio managed to that strategy. Similarly, the net-of-fees performance for a composite that includes carve-outs that is presented to a prospective client for a multi-asset strategy portfolio must be calculated using an investment management fee that is representative of the investment management fees that would be charged for a multi-asset strategy portfolio managed according to that multi-asset strategy.

For example, assume Firm B manages a balanced strategy that contains both an equity and a fixed-income component, and the firm wants to carve out the equity component to create an equity composite. Firm B charges a 0.50% investment management fee for its balanced strategy. The equity strategy will charge a 0.75% investment management fee. When calculating and presenting net-of-fees returns to prospective clients interested in the equity strategy, the firm must use 0.75% as the investment management fee when calculating net-of-fees returns.

Wrap Fee

Provision 2.A.48

When calculating returns to be presented to a WRAP FEE PROSPECTIVE CLIENT, returns MUST be calculated net of the entire WRAP FEE. This is applicable to all WRAP FEE PORTFOLIOS in the COMPOSITE as well as any non–WRAP FEE PORTFOLIOS in the COMPOSITE.

Discussion

A wrap fee is a type of bundled fee specific to a particular investment product. The wrap fee is charged by a wrap fee sponsor for investment management services and typically includes associated transaction costs that cannot be separately identified. Wrap fees can be all-inclusive, asset-based fees, and they may include a combination of investment management fees, transaction costs, custody fees, and/or administrative fees.

When presenting performance to a wrap fee prospective client, performance must be shown net of the entire wrap fee. This requirement applies to all wrap fee portfolios in the composite as well as any non–wrap fee portfolios that are included in the composite.

If a firm has not managed actual wrap fee portfolios in a specific strategy, the firm may create a history from that strategy's non–wrap fee composite. The wrap fee performance history for that specific strategy may be calculated by using that strategy's gross-of-fees non–wrap fee composite history reduced by the highest total wrap fee charged to the client (end user) by the wrap fee sponsor for the strategy (product), resulting in net-of-fees wrap fee performance.

It is up to the firm to determine the appropriate highest wrap fee to deduct. This highest wrap fee should be obtained from the prospective wrap fee sponsor and should be comparable to the investment mandate, objective, or strategy of the wrap fee composite.

It is recognized that, when starting with the gross-of-fees non–wrap fee composite history, the gross-of-fees performance already reflects the deduction of actual transaction costs incurred. By then reducing the composite performance by the highest total wrap fee, which includes a portion attributable to transaction costs, performance will reflect the deduction of transaction costs twice (actual transaction costs and a portion of the highest wrap fee). If the firm can identify the portion of the highest total wrap fee attributable to transaction costs, or if the firm can estimate appropriate transaction costs, the firm may first calculate performance reflecting the deduction of both transaction costs and the highest wrap fee. The firm may then increase this result by the identifiable portion of the wrap fee attributable to actual or estimated transaction costs in order to compute a net-of-fees return.

To assist prospective clients and their understanding of the fees charged in these situations, when presenting gross-of-fees returns, firms must disclose if other fees are deducted in addition to the transaction costs. When presenting net-of-fees returns, firms must disclose if any other fees are deducted in addition to the investment management fees and transaction costs.

"Pure" gross-of-fees returns, which represent the return on investments that is not reduced by any transaction costs incurred during the period, are permitted only as supplemental information in a GIPS Composite Report and must be clearly labelled as such.

The following table describes the various returns that can be calculated for wrap fee portfolios:

Examples of Gross-of-Fees and Net-of-Fees Calculations

Non-wrap Composite	**Presenting to Current Wrap Fee Sponsors and Clients When Unbundling Wrap Fee**	**Presenting to Prospective Wrap Fee Sponsors and Clients**
Return on investments ("pure gross")[a]	Return on investments ("pure gross")[a]	Return on investments ("pure gross")[a]
– Transaction Costs	– Portion of wrap fee that includes transaction costs that can be segregated *Or* – Estimated transaction costs	
Gross-of-fees return	**Gross-of-fees return**	
– Investment management fee	– Portion of wrap fee that includes an investment management fee that can be segregated *Or* – Model investment management fee	– Model Wrap Fee *Or* – Actual Wrap Fee
Net-of-fees return	**Net-of-fees return**	
– Administrative Fee	– Remaining portion of wrap fee (administrative fees, if any)	
Client return[b]	**Client return**[b]	**Gross-of-fees return** **Net-of-fees return** **Client return**[c]

[a] Although the "pure gross" return is not required or recommended by the GIPS standards, it may be presented as supplemental information.

[b] The client return is not required by the GIPS standards and is presented here as additional information that may be helpful for existing clients.

[c] For wrap fee portfolios, the net-of-fees return is equal to the client return. If the firm does not have the ability to unbundle the wrap fee or estimate transaction costs, the net-of-fees return will also equal the gross-of-fees return.

Side Pockets and Subscription Lines of Credit

Provision 2.A.49

All COMPOSITE and POOLED FUND returns MUST include the effect of any discretionary SIDE POCKETS held by PORTFOLIOS in the COMPOSITE or the POOLED FUND.[27]

Discussion

A side pocket is a segregated investment that is used mainly in alternative investment pooled funds, such as hedge funds, funds of funds, and other alternative investment funds, to separate illiquid or distressed assets from other, more liquid investments or to segregate investments held for a special purpose from other investments. Side pockets are typically not available for investing for new pooled fund investors that invest after the side pocket has been created. All composite and pooled fund returns must include the effect of any discretionary side pockets held by portfolios in the composite or the pooled fund. The fact that future investors will not be participating in the performance of the side pocket is not a valid argument to exclude the side pocket from composite or pooled fund performance.

Firms may choose to also present returns without side pockets. Prospective clients and investors may be interested in the performance history without the effect of the side pocket because they will not be participating in the performance of the side pocket going forward.

A firm may exclude the effect of a non-discretionary side pocket on composite or pooled fund returns, just as firms may exclude non-discretionary assets from a portfolio's performance. A side pocket can be classified as non-discretionary only when all of the following criteria are met:

- The side pocket is segregated in a separate sub-portfolio (e.g., at the custodian bank or in the portfolio management system of the firm).
- The side-pocketed assets are no longer considered in the asset allocation and portfolio investment process.
- There are no investment decisions for the side-pocketed assets, except for monitoring and liquidating.
- There are no or reduced investment management fees charged on the side-pocketed assets.

A side pocket created at the express direction of a client may be considered non-discretionary and excluded from the performance of the composite or pooled fund, as if it were an unmanaged asset.

[27] REQUIRED for periods beginning on or after 1 October 2012.

Provision 2.A.50

When calculating MONEY-WEIGHTED RETURNS for COMPOSITES and POOLED FUNDS without the SUBSCRIPTION LINES OF CREDIT, the FIRM MUST include the cash flows from the SUBSCRIPTION LINES OF CREDIT.[28]

Discussion

A subscription line of credit is a loan facility that is usually put in place to facilitate administration when firms are calling for funds from investors. It is secured by limited partner commitments.

Subscription lines of credit are being used by more firms and for longer periods. These lines of credit can have a significant effect on returns. As has been widely discussed in the industry, there has also been a lack of consistency in return calculations when lines of credit are used. The purpose of Provision 2.A.50 is to help standardize the calculation of returns for composites and pooled funds that include a subscription line of credit, thereby increasing the comparability of returns from one firm to another.

Firms that use subscription lines of credit must calculate and present the since-inception money-weighted return (MWR) that includes the subscription line of credit. Firms are required to also calculate a since-inception MWR that does not include the subscription line of credit unless the subscription line of credit has the following two characteristics:

- The principal was repaid within 120 days using committed capital drawn down through a capital call.
- No principal was used to fund distributions.

The following example illustrates the MWRs calculated with and without the subscription line of credit. Note that the return with the subscription line of credit, which some may think of as being a levered return, is the return for which the period for the performance calculation is shortened, resulting in a higher return in an up market and a lower return in a down market. We refer to this as the return "with" the subscription line of credit because the period could not be shortened unless the subscription line of credit was used. The return without the subscription line of credit assumes the line of credit was not used and capital was called to fund investments. In the following example, we can think of the return without the subscription line of credit as being the return on the investment, whereas the return with the subscription line of credit is the return the investor (limited partner) would earn if a subscription line of credit was used.

[28] REQUIRED for MONEY-WEIGHTED RETURNS for periods ending on or after 31 December 2020.

	A	B	C	D
1			Net MWR	Net MWR
2			With	Without
3			Subscription	Subscription
4			Line of Credit	Line of Credit
5				
6	**Date**	**Transaction Type**	**Cash Flow**	**Cash Flow**
7	6-Jan-2020	Subscription LOC Drawdown		(1,000,000)
8	1-Jul-2020	Subscription LOC Drawdown		(500,000)
9	1-Oct-2020	Subscription LOC Drawdown		(500,000)
10	15-Dec-2020	Capital Call	(2,000,000)	
11	1-Oct-2021	Capital Call	(1,000,000)	(1,000,000)
12	31-Dec-2021	Ending Fair Value	3,500,000	3,500,000
13		SI-MWR	21.47%	13.28%

When using the XIRR formula in Excel, firms must include the first cell that contains the first capital call or subscription line of credit drawdown. For example, the XIRR formula for the Net MWR with Subscription Line of Credit is =XIRR(C10:C12,A10:A12,0.1), where C10:C12 reflects the cash flows and ending value. A10:A12 reflects the dates of the cash flows and ending value, and the 0.1 is a guess of what the IRR will be. If firms omit the guess, Excel assumes it is 10% or 0.1. Generally, a guess is not required. Note that the XIRR annualizes the result. If calculating for a period that is less than a year, firms will need to calculate the non-annualized return. See Provision 2.A.12 for the formula to calculate the non-annualized return.

Firms that are required to present returns both with and without the subscription line of credit must present comparable returns in GIPS Reports. If presenting gross returns, the firm must present gross returns with the subscription line of credit and without the subscription line of credit. The same is true for net returns. If presenting net returns, the firm must present net returns with the subscription line of credit and without the subscription line of credit.

When calculating returns without the subscription line of credit, firms may also exclude interest expense associated with the subscription line of credit. Firms should consider disclosing whether interest expense and other subscription line of credit costs are or are not reflected in the return without the subscription line of credit.

2.B. Input Data and Calculation Methodology—Recommendations

Provision 2.B.1

The FIRM SHOULD value PORTFOLIOS on the date of all EXTERNAL CASH FLOWS.

Discussion

To improve the accuracy of time-weighted performance calculations, the GIPS standards have gradually increased the minimum required frequency of portfolio valuation for many portfolio types from quarterly, to monthly, to the date of all large cash flows for periods beginning on or after 1 January 2010. Best practice, however, is to value portfolios on the date of all external cash flows. Firms are encouraged to create a policy to value portfolios on the date of all external cash flows as part of the composite-specific valuation policy where possible.

Provision 2.B.2

Valuations SHOULD be obtained from a qualified independent third party.

Discussion

The quality of valuations used as inputs to calculate performance has a significant effect on the accuracy of portfolio and composite returns; therefore, it is important that the valuations used are accurate. It is recommended that firms obtain valuations from an independent source because a third party can provide the most objective investment valuations. In most instances, obtaining valuations from an independent third party is considered to be a best practice. A firm claiming compliance with the GIPS standards is responsible for its claim of compliance and must ensure that the valuations obtained from a third party can be used to satisfy the requirements of the GIPS standards.

Provision 2.B.3

ACCRUAL ACCOUNTING SHOULD be used for dividends (as of the ex-dividend date).

Discussion

Accrual accounting determines the correct economic value of the portfolio assets and allows the recording of financial transactions as they come into existence rather than when they are paid or settled. It is recommended that dividends be recognized when earned on ex-date (accrual basis) versus when paid (cash basis).

Provision 2.B.4

The FIRM SHOULD accrue INVESTMENT MANAGEMENT FEES.

Discussion

Investment management fees are the fees payable to the investment management firm for the ongoing management of a portfolio. They are typically asset based (based on a percentage of assets), performance based (based on the portfolio's performance either on an absolute basis or relative to a benchmark), or a combination of the two, but they may take other forms as well. Investment management fees also include carried interest.

To calculate a net-of-fees return for a portfolio or composite, the gross-of-fees return must be reduced by investment management fees. To calculate a pooled fund net return, the pooled fund gross return must be reduced by investment management fees as well as by administrative fees and other costs. To reflect the most accurate net-of-fees return, investment management fees should be accrued when possible. Accrual accounting allows the recording of financial transactions as they come into existence rather when they are paid or settled. Net-of-fees returns can be skewed if investment management fees are reflected in the calculation as they are paid, particularly when portfolio values change significantly.

Provision 2.B.5

Returns SHOULD be calculated net of non-reclaimable withholding taxes on dividends, interest, and capital gains. Reclaimable withholding taxes SHOULD be accrued.

Discussion

Global investing requires recognition of the tax consequences of investing in different countries. The GIPS standards recommend that performance be reported net of non-reclaimable withholding taxes on dividends, interest, and capital gains. Some countries allow certain types of foreign investors to reclaim a portion of the foreign withholding taxes that are paid. These reclaimable foreign withholding taxes may be credited back to the investor at a later date. It is recommended that reclaimable foreign withholding taxes be accrued, meaning that the refund for reclaimable withholding taxes should be recorded when the reclaimable withholding taxes become a receivable owed to the firm, rather than when the refund is actually received.

Provision 2.B.6

The FIRM SHOULD incorporate the following hierarchy into its policies and procedures for determining FAIR VALUE for PORTFOLIO investments on a COMPOSITE-specific or POOLED FUND–specific basis.

a. Investments MUST be valued using objective, observable, unadjusted quoted market prices for identical investments in active markets on the measurement date, if available. If such prices are not available, then investments SHOULD be valued using;

b. Objective, observable quoted market prices for similar investments in active markets. If such prices are not available or appropriate, then investments SHOULD be valued using;

c. Quoted prices for identical or similar investments in markets that are not active (markets in which there are few transactions for the investment, the prices are not current, or price quotations vary substantially over time and/or between market makers). If such prices are not available or appropriate, then investments SHOULD be valued based on;

d. Market-based inputs, other than quoted prices, that are observable for the investment. If such inputs are not available or appropriate, then investments SHOULD be valued based on;

e. Subjective, unobservable inputs for the investment where markets are not active at the measurement date. Unobservable inputs SHOULD be used to measure FAIR VALUE only when observable inputs and prices are not available or appropriate. Unobservable inputs reflect the FIRM'S own assumptions about the assumptions that market participants would use in pricing the investment and SHOULD be developed based on the best information available under the circumstances.

Discussion

The GIPS standards include a recommended valuation hierarchy as presented in Provision 2.B.6. It is recommended that firms incorporate this hierarchy into their policies for determining fair value for portfolio investments on a composite-specific or pooled fund–specific basis. For further information regarding fair valuation and the frequency of internal and external valuation requirements, please refer to Provision 2.A.19.

Provision 2.B.7

The FIRM SHOULD use GROSS-OF-FEES returns when calculating risk measures.

Discussion

Acknowledging that there are many acceptable calculation variations for various risk measures, the GIPS standards do not prescribe a specific methodology for calculating risk measures. It is recommended, however, that gross-of-fees returns be used when calculating risk measures. It is recommended that firms use gross-of-fees returns because these are not affected by investment management fees, which may introduce additional variability of returns.

Firms are required to select a calculation methodology, on a composite-specific or pooled fund-specific basis, for each risk measure presented in a GIPS Report. They must document the chosen calculation methodology in their policies and procedures, and then consistently apply the methodology selected.

Provision 2.B.8

PRIVATE MARKET INVESTMENTS SHOULD have an EXTERNAL VALUATION at least once every 12 months.

Discussion

For periods beginning on or after 1 January 2020, it is recommended that private market investments have an external valuation at least once every 12 months. (This is a requirement for real estate investments in a real estate open-end fund. Real estate investments not in a real estate open-end fund must have an external valuation at least once every 12 months, unless client agreements stipulate a less frequent external valuation, or be subject to an annual financial statement audit. See Provisions 2.A.43 and 2.A.44.)

Those evaluating a firm's private market investments, including prospective clients or investors, typically prefer an external valuation because it is independent, unbiased, and an "expert" estimate of value that is perceived by the marketplace to be more reliable than an internal valuation.

An external valuation is an assessment of value performed by an independent third party who is a professionally designated or certified commercial property valuer or appraiser. In markets where these professionals are unavailable, steps must be taken to ensure that only qualified independent property valuers or appraisers are used. For additional information regarding an external valuation, please refer to Provision 2.A.45.

Made in the USA
Monee, IL
05 November 2026

67843127R10046